DOMINICA,
THE DARK ISLAND

Also by Michael Tritico:
Stars Above My Hearse

DOMINICA, THE DARK ISLAND

A Misadventure in Eden with Zombies, Rastafarians, and Other Revolutionaries

MICHAEL TRITICO

iUniverse, Inc.
Bloomington

Dominica, the Dark Island
A Misadventure in Eden with Zombies, Rastafarians, and Other Revolutionaries

iUniverse books may be ordered through booksellers or by contacting:

iUniverse
1663 Liberty Drive
Bloomington, IN 47403
www.iuniverse.com
1-800-Authors (1-800-288-4677)

ISBN: 978-1-4759-2422-0 (sc)
ISBN: 978-1-4759-2424-4 (hc)
ISBN: 978-1-4759-2423-7 (e)

Printed in the United States of America

iUniverse rev. date: 05/22/2012

To: Claire Charleaux (my favorite isomer), Lili Grand Bois of Quebec, Gaspar of St. Lucia, the Rastafarians of Dominica, Magdoweel and the Indian River Boatsmen of Portsmouth

"There are sharks in those waters, Mike, and they don't all have fins that you can see; do you understand?" Harry Tubbs, Lake Charles, 1980

TABLE OF CONTENTS

PART ONE
The Roseau Situation

PART TWO
Portsmouth — An Entirely Different Situation, Almost —

PREFACE

I have not been back to Dominica in over thirty years. I wrote this book in 1981, shortly after the events happened, but its publication was blocked by people who did not want my viewpoints aired.

You might want to do an Internet search for "Operation Red Dog" which, although I was unaware of its existence during my time on Dominica, explains much of what happened to me and to the other unfortunate Americans, some of whom who did not escape the righteous fury that spread through the island homelands. Suppression of truth prevailed at that time. Here at home in the United States most of you never heard most of what happened. That was by design. Such hiding of and misportrayals of our government's clandestine shenanigans abroad is not just shameful, it is traitorous.

Whatever you might find on the Internet about "Operation Red Dog," having been a plot concocted by radical racists intent on taking over a newly-independent nation, consider instead my theory:

An American president had made bold statements urging the world to fight terrorism, to not let their nations provide aid and comfort to anyone who might threaten some other country. He contended that the United States would lead the way; should any terrorists ever try to use our country as a home base, his administration would surely take every measure to destroy the terrorists and protect our fellow nations.

What, then, would have been the next step in making sure that the world had paid attention to that message? Surely it might have been more than just coincidental that someone convinced some fringe elements of the Ku Klux Klan that Dominica was "easy pickins." Not to be confused with the larger Dominican Republic, Dominica was a newly independent small island nation rich with timber resources that could provide an immediate cash return on the world market. It was rich also in "cheap," (as in slave-ready) labor.

The fringe element must have taken the bait and swallowed it deeply because they got as far as the dock in New Orleans aboard a chartered vessel, ready to leave for their invasion and world recognition, a resurrection of dormant Nazi dreams.

Continuing with my theory: The someone who had cast out the bait made certain that it was swallowed, then alerted the FBI who intercepted the invasion here at home. The someone also alerted the State Department who dutifully alerted the threatened nation but also reassured the country's new female prime minister that the American president meant what he had said, that no terrorists would be allowed to harm our friends. Just to be sure, though, they told her that should anyone from Texas, Louisiana, or Quebec, (homes of the alleged invaders), happen to slip through and arrive in Dominica, just give him a call...the Great Communicator...

Now, in a new century, I have visited Dominica in cyberspace. The Internet shows the island's beauty, unchanged. It shows facilities greatly-improved. There does seem to have been a significant progression toward a better quality of life for the people who live there. I am very glad that those blessings have happened.

Nevertheless, rather than change what I wrote during a time when I was obviously discouraged by my misadventure on Dominica, I believe that it might be useful for people to have an old account like mine to use for comparisons and contrasts that might now be made showing how key circumstances on Dominica and in the United States have changed or have remained stagnant.

Let the shipwreck that one can now see on the Internet by doing a search for "shipwreck, Portsmouth, Dominica" stand as a reminder of dreams frustrated by greed and intrigue. Let the cargo we had to jettison continue to be recycled endlessly in the sea as nourishment for the resurrection of virtue, not for human greed or political power.

I certainly hope that a sad old saying I heard more than once while I was on the island has turned out to be completely and irrevocably obsolete: "Oh, Dominica, Dominica, you never change, you never change."

I certainly hope that America will change back to what its forefathers intended, back to the America I so admired when I was a child.

ACKNOWLEDGMENTS

My sister Mary Jane has patiently expressed insights, typed the manuscript, and made the many necessary changes in punctuation. My brother Frank has supported this effort and many of my other endeavors through the years. All members of my family and all my friends have tolerated my idiosyncrasies, forgiven me for my flaws, and tried to encourage me to do things in better ways.

My deepest gratitude is to the Creator for always providing a way for me to survive, to escape, and for lending me people to make escape and survival possible. On Dominica those people were each right where and when they had to be for all our sakes. I thank them now and always for their righteousness.

PART ONE

THE ROSEAU SITUATION

Chapter One

Green Lights All the Way

"Why don't one of you people come along and set me free?"
Jim Morrison, The Doors, Los Angeles, 1967

Like many people who had reveled in the special time of the late sixties only to see the refreshing spirit of that time collapse, my life had become miserable, again. I had begun to feel so bound by circumstances that my bones ached as certainly as if they had been fettered with hot ribbed wires. My breath was being caught in thickening webs of moisture. My channels seemed to be clogging, drying, clotting, crying, rotting. I had become, again, physically ill from an intensely dynamic form of stagnation. Still, I felt needed, for once, needed as a warrior in the Louisiana environmental war that I had helped actuate.

After several years of high stress involving confrontations over public health and ecological problems caused by hazardous wastes and other offspring of the depletable-resource-based economic system that had overcome Louisiana, I finally and firmly decided that I would have to leave for a while if I were to just survive. I would have to get away from all the chaos I had stepped into, voluntarily. I would have to get away from everything that needed me right then because it would all surely need me even more later. If I were to have any "later," I knew that I would have to leave, for a little while, and maybe for a little while longer. I really needed a break, just a vacation, some time to myself, a nice deserted beach, some fresh fruit, a clear mountain stream, a friend to talk to when I wanted her. I really needed a Day of Rest; (so did the other officers of our little environmental group, RESTORE. Even the "mystery member," Claire, usually the fearless voice of aggressive direct action during our environmental strategy sessions, agreed that the wisest course, temporarily, had to be a controlled retreat.)

In Lake Charles we were surrounded by heroes, but the horrors were becoming almost overwhelming. We all decided to take our breaks immediately and simultaneously, especially from each other. One went west, one went north, I decided to go southeast.

Where is southeast of the Louisiana coastal zone? Where is beautiful, quiet, peaceful, ecologically fascinating, mangoed, mountained, green, green, green, and southeast? I went to the libraries and started checking them out, books and islands. Which would I choose? Whichever one it would be, I figured that I had earned my fare even though I had never figured out how to cash in the cosmic paychecks, those ethereal rewards that were what seemed to have been all that I had been working for during most of the preceding five years.

I quit wondering how or whether I would ever get the money to go to the Caribbean. I just had faith that it would happen, in time. Most of the information available in the libraries was at least a year old and included warnings that prices were rising. The travel books suggested that I write to various national boards of tourism for current prices of things such as guesthouses, airport taxes and other things I had never heard of, so I wrote to those boards. I even wrote to an island newspaper and asked for copies of their latest issues correctly reasoning that I might get some important insight into present realities. (Perhaps I should have subscribed for a year, read carefully, and then decided: "perhaps this, perhaps that, perhaps nothing...")

I am certain that I did my "homework" better than would have most tourists or business travelers. I tried as hard as I could to get every scrap of information I could get about every Caribbean island I could. I tried as hard as I could, but my guardian angels could see that I was like a very nearsighted armadillo sniffing the meandering crack in the pavement oblivious to the eighteen-wheelers approaching from all directions.

Some of the islands I read about seemed to be merged well into the twentieth century, too well for me to be able to expect a peaceful retreat from chaos. Others seemed to be waiting to move into a time of improvement, rational prosperity with the chance for betterment without loss of the old renewable-resource-based way of life. One of those insightful places seemed to be Dominica, Sunday Island, named by Christopher Columbus for the Day of Rest, the day he found it.

Dominica is an Eastern Caribbean island, thirty miles long and sixteen miles across. It is rugged, covered with a lush climax rain forest, sparsely inhabited except for dense coastal settlements. It is quite beautiful. There are bird species unknown anywhere else on earth; there are hundreds of tumbling mountain streams, supposedly one for every day of the year. The island is a giant volcano which has erupted from the ocean floor at the point of convergence of two suboceanic continental plates. Dominica rises so abruptly from the sea and climbs to such a height so quickly, almost a mile, that the nearly constant tradewinds, coming in from the northeast, saturated with water vapor picked up in their thousands of miles of marine passage, must lift. They must, as if on a ramp, climb the windward slopes. They must collide with the jungle. Squeezed into and around its trees and vines the clouds must clamber up the island's earthy and rocky walls. A steep mile higher into the cooler realm of our atmosphere, the tradewinds collapse over the pinnacle of the island; depleted of their energy, chilled by their altitude, freed by their expansion and released from pressure, those tradewinds must let go of their moisture. It rains on Dominica. It rains almost all the time.

I became convinced that the island to go to, for me, for the former Park Ranger, former Ranger-Naturalist, and former (I hoped) radical-alarmist-eco-freak (as the Louisiana corporate community had tried to label me), would be that island advertised as the "Nature Island of the Caribbean," Dominica. Any place that had set aside a great percentage of its landmass as a National Park always to be preserved, had to have the most farsighted national government on the planet.

I saw that there were things that might make a day of life easier on Dominica, things that I might be able to help bring about, things that should not be too hard to accomplish. For example, I saw that there was a problem with distribution of electricity which would mean that areas beyond the capital would likely be devoid of refrigeration. I considered large-scale ideas such as ways to use the tumbling streams to generate electricity without using dams. Drawing my mind back to a more practical level, I considered stopgap measures such as something that had just been announced, cartons of milk that would not require refrigeration because they had been irradiated.

My thoughts gained more and more energy the more I read, the more I realized I could be on the threshold of a frontier of opportunities like the frontiers of opportunities experienced by my forefathers when they came to America. I saw problems, but I also saw solutions. I saw the chance to make things better, much better, for many, many people. I saw a chance to help the clearheaded people make their Dominica (a perfect yet challenging habitat) into a model of diligent human movement toward perfection, a model the world would be able to see, scale up, and follow.

The information from source after source said that Dominica was an island of rainbows: "Mists rise gently from lush green valleys and fall softly over blue green peaks. Rivers framed by banks of giant ferns rush and tumble to the sea. Trees sprout orchids...This most naturally beautiful of all islands..."

I decided then to go to Dominica as soon as I could, as soon as the wherewithal arrived. Then, sure enough, the earth fell in, actually. Lake Peignur near Abbeville, Louisiana, November 20, 1980, emptied into the hole formed by an oil well puncture of a salt dome cavern, one of Louisiana's endless fiascoes. That event gave me another short consulting job. I made a little money. I seemed to have nothing but green lights, "GO!" signs, bright beacons drawing me toward peace in a Caribbean paradise.

I flew off to Dominica. I flew off to the most poverty-stricken ghetto in Paradise. Surely, had I been on that island with just you, Claire Charleaux, I would have been on the Nature Island of the Caribbean, our own paradise...coconuts, parrots, waterfalls, rainbows!

You were not with me. A hundred thousand prisoners and I were trapped on Sunday Island without a day of rest, every day just like the rest, every day a struggle to decide, a struggle to act, to find a move, to make that move, and a struggle to get out of the way of the equal but opposite reaction stimulated by that move.

What was it on Dominica that stepped its way into every good situation and turned it into chaos? What aberrant mind infected and spoiled the wise plans and noble projects of the sages of Dominica? What force was never mentioned in any of the materials I studied during my research, what force that seemed to be able to command and to destroy, yet never show itself?

The windward side of the island and all its mountaintops seem eternally dark, enshrouded by a blanket of tears. It rains on Dominica. It rains almost all the time. Dominica, for me, at times was a dark, dark island.

Whose fault is it that nothing seems to work on Dominica, nothing except Nature and its greatest adversary? Whose fault is it that real, advanced humans are so fully overwhelmed by invisible, inhuman, horridly evil and absolutely unreal primitive forces, unreal except in the minds of people and their governments? Whose fault is it anywhere on earth?

If there is a place where we can find out, it is Dominica.

CHAPTER TWO

THE REAL WORLD

"As long as you're out there anyway,
We might as well get you back on your feet again.
(Who knows, you might just touch someone.)
We've got to get from here to there, eventually."
Steppenwolf, Los Angeles, late sixties

I left all my troubles in Lake Charles. I made sure that no one would be able to precede or follow me to my secret refuge unless and until I gave the signal. If there were to continue to be a constantly increasing spectrum of variables in my life, I felt that I had earned at least the right to know whether or not the complications were being self-generated, were of significance just to me, were complications that were necessary, that were just nuisances, that were fair or unfair...I felt that I had earned at least the right to cover my tracks and split for a while, the same right my pal Claire had sought to earn for so long.

It was a nice Easter. My two little boys who lived in New Orleans with their mother hunted eggs in Hammond. The family canoed, cooked spaghetti, studied for law exams, and saw a Pryor movie; the family held together for a full three-day Easter holiday and going-away-scene. I thought of telling them how ill I was, that I was convinced that it could not be long before something major would give way physiologically if I kept up in the same way that I had been living for the past few years. I thought of telling them that my only chance to RESTORE myself would be to run and get some good air and water, fun exercise, pleasure food... I decided to condense it and tell them I needed a break.

It was very hard to leave the boys, the family, Claire, and friends as I was actively attempting to convince them that I was really leaving, maybe for good. In Calcasieu Parish there were few tears. At the airport in New Orleans, however, one of the boys cried. I almost did. Another five seconds of good-bye and I also would I have cried for sure; I really would miss them. One close friend just refused to write—we talked on the phone—we really missed each other. Changing one's life to sustain it can sometimes be almost fatal.

From New Orleans I caught the 9 p.m. Eastern 727 for Atlanta. I saw distant thunderstorms from above. Back on the ground I rode my first subway in the Atlanta airport. After midnight I caught the L-1011 jumbojet to San Juan. It was an amazing machine and an amazing concept. The L-1011 carried over three hundred of us in luxury seven miles above the earth. There was disco music in optional earphones, no extra charge, very American, very confident. There were many stewardesses, and they all seemed to be very happy workers. The passengers were a contented group even though we had been herded like sheep and given no choice in seating arrangements. I noticed that about a third of these San Juan bound people were Puerto Rican-looking. They seemed to be neither happy nor sad about going home.

During the flight there were a few ruffles in the air, but otherwise it felt like the giant plane was being flown by a robot—the control was rock-steady in all dimensions. Still, as we descended, I had the same tense and artificial feeling I had when I used to land flying machines, the feeling I probably always will have thanks to a skydiving accident (the one I had when I did not do things the jumpmaster Henri's way). It is a feeling that the guardian angels are stepping back to let me learn something the hard way.

The five-hour layover in the San Juan airport was boring. I watched people. There was a large variety of people; many were Spanish-speaking, many of those were blond. I watched planes come and go. I was impatient.

I saw clouds hanging over distant mountains. I saw my first coconut trees on a beach beyond the airport. I waited for the ticket counters to reopen for the day.

My ticket was written to allow me to island-hop between San Juan and Dominica. I had requested that arrangement so that I would be able to see most of the Lesser Antilles and even land on a few of them. I would fly the Puerto Rican airline Prinair part of the way, then transfer to LIAT, a Caribbean airline that flies into Dominica. The first of many strange things that were to happen to me began at the Prinair counter that morning. The ticket agent asked my body weight and to weigh my carry-ons because it was a small plane. Then he picked up the phone and in Spanish gave someone my computer-assigned seat number, passport number, my name, some quick phrase I did not understand, and then a reference to *diable.* I began wondering what that garbled phrase had been, perhaps a reference to the landlord, Satan, at what they believed would be my ultimate destination, Hades? I thought not, hoped not; I hoped that they were talking about the ultimate destination on my ticket, the Melville Hall Airport which lies in the evening shadow of Morne Diablotin, the tallest mountain on Dominica, Mountain of the Imps.

As we were leaving Puerto Rico, I noticed lots of open land, many square miles of very pleasant, pastoral countryside. I was surprised at that since I had heard so much about people leaving Puerto Rico and moving to the slums of the cities up north. I wondered what could be so bad down in those warm, green fields that could drive millions of people thousands of miles north into freezing ghettos. I thought back to the hundred Puerto Ricans that had been on the airbus coming down with me earlier that morning, and I guessed that maybe they were coming back home to warn the next batch not to go north, maybe.

I quit thinking, I saw a beautiful green ocean beneath me. I saw the green, plenty of it all around, and I felt better immediately. The green became a beautiful deep blue out to my side, and the sky's blue touched it at the horizon. I felt invigorated yet soothed, and I wanted to take a picture because I knew that we could not fly forever. I got back much of my lost vigor in just those few hours that I was soaring above the sea.

Prinair was chaotic, but they got the job done and usually on time. Flying the world's ugliest aircraft, the DeHavilland Heron, a four micro-engined, eighteen-passenger set of disproportionate contradictions, Prinair's Heron hopscotched swiftly and gracefully from island to island. Our pilots let us off at each stop to give us a chance to use the restrooms, send postcards, get a drink, or just stroll around so that we could measure the changes in culture and customs as we proceeded southward.

I looked forward to restoring the rest of my strength by being able to sit on the slopes at Mount Joy on Dominica, to sit watching the western sea at sunset with the old man Stephen Haws, author of *Mount Joy* waiting patiently for that strange phenomenon (the "emerald drop") that I had read about in his book and heard about one time from one of my science teachers, an old glider pilot, Colonel Deaton. The "emerald drop" is a momentary flash of green in the sky just after sunset as the earth's atmosphere acts as a prism separating the sun's light as it bends back over the horizon.

I had tasted one kind of cosmic green, the sight of the ocean below, and my appetite for another kind was becoming ravenous. I had become certain that my inner drives were no longer to be suppressed but that I should cut them loose completely, once and for all, yet I had not yet regained the strength to do it. I thought: "How absurd, how truly absurd you are! You do not even have the strength to surrender! Not even the capacity remaining to let your own body and mind save themselves even though they are fighting to do it and to tell you how to do it! How absurd you really are!" I realized that I was isomerizing again (my own phrase for something psychiatry stacks up books and books about, physics calls resonance, art calls the Muse, it is all just isomerism, sometimes controlled, sometimes not, sometimes orderly, sometimes entropic, the instinct for oneness, unity with the Original).

The plane began to descend. I saw a giant two-bladed windmill on one of the Virgin Islands as we came into St. Thomas. I felt more comfortable with this landing, reassured that the best thoughts of man could survive in isolated places, that man himself might survive if he would not clot himself up into vulnerable knots of millions upon millions of tangling, struggling other men. St. Thomas seemed peaceful, I got "good vibes," and I thought of just staying. No, I am on my way to the Nature Island of the Caribbean, I told myself. I am on my way, and I am going to get there—besides, this island looks a little dry for someone from South Louisiana. Flying out of St. Thomas I photographed Charlotte Amalie which looked like a peaceful and pleasant place.

We flew over some small islands, places that looked like southern California seacoasts complete with scattered condominia and hundreds of sailboats. The sea became even more emerald with the deep blue water far off to the east. The next stop was St. Maarten, a Dutch and French island, a free-trade zone. There was a big old DC-6 parked on the flight line, no numbers (or, as my fantasy went, tons of numbers—they were just hidden inside instead of being painted on the wings). We refueled and took off again. The scalloped southern end of the island looked like a perfect place for some marine science grad students to go study "Form/Process Relationships."

I became convinced that I had made a correct decision to use the low-flying Prinair route between San Juan and Antigua. We had a very pretty flight over the small, dry Leeward islands: St. Bart's, Nevis, St. Kitts, Saba, and Montserrat.

CHAPTER THREE

———

ANTIGUA

"Nature's castles have no walls."
Lawrence Cyral Cooper, Merryville, Louisiana
Sometime during the Depression

As we approached Antigua, I saw that it had a typical oil refinery spoiling its otherwise pretty face. The grease was oozing down into the sea. Pits of tar looked like blackheads the same as they look on Louisiana's face. I felt needed again, but this time it was not a nice feeling; this was not my home. Let Antigua restore itself, I was too tired. I was glad that I had anticipated the "jet lag" that had now become a real addition to my illness. My ticket had an overnight layover built into it, and Antigua was the place I had planned to stay that night since it was English-speaking and the travel guides had been fairly complimentary.

They had also mentioned a small casino. Since I knew that I was barely going to be able to afford the trip and would have little spending money unless I could find a job on Dominica or some other good fortune, I had considered during my planning of the trip that I might as well lay over on some island with a casino. (In the sixties I worked for a while in a Nevada casino, later making a good living for a few weeks as a freelance blackjack player. I had retired quickly from that work when it became just a little too enjoyable as I realized that I was on the verge of becoming addicted, something that I did not want to happen. Even in Nevada where the rules are more in favor of the players and less in favor of the house than they are in many of the world's casinos, an addicted gambler, no matter how efficient he is, will lose in the long run. I do not like to lose.) Anyway, when I was setting up the ticket, I built in a layover that would give me a casino option to at least check out.

We landed and were directed to the customs gates. The agent was pleasant and quiet. He asked where I would be staying, and I said that I didn't know yet but that if he knew of an inexpensive place... so he recommended with a twinkle in his eye, Cornelia's Castle. It was a good recommendation. He must have been a very sharp character reader. At Cornelia's I met some fascinating West Indian intellectuals—Roy, an engineer from Guyana, Kenneth and Vaughn, who were journalists from St. Vincent, and Cornelia herself—even her staff members were strong thinkers and very articulate, and the food was delicious.

Cornelia's Castle was a guesthouse, not a hotel. I was unfamiliar with the concept of guesthouses, but I am glad that I was introduced to them on Antigua. Each guest had his own room which was very comfortable, clean, and private. There were several bathrooms to choose from and even though they were at the end of the hall and to be shared among all the guests, everyone's schedules were so different that there was never any conflict or waiting. All guests did meet in the dining room for breakfast and supper and that gave everyone a chance to meet and talk. I quickly realized that the West Indians had developed that conversational mechanism that they were using to keep each other up to date on current happenings across the islands while most tourists continued to isolate themselves in the expensive concrete hotels. My conversations at Cornelia's Castle may have saved my life later; they certainly gave me a much more accurate briefing on the realities of the Caribbean than I had gotten from my readings. I listened to what Roy, Kenneth, Cornelia, and the others had to say, and I heard common sense fine-tuned for the local pace and politics. That local pace was even slower than it was at home, and the politics was even more complex. They also alerted me to the fact that politics was one thing where the pace had recently become more and more accelerated. I thought to myself: "Guess what! I always seem to hit town at about the same time! Guess the Creator considers me a trained factor of some kind—guess it would be 'Hopeless Romance, here I go again, another round in the ring with the power brokers,' that is, if I stayed on Antigua."

I asked them: "What about Dominica?"

They shook their heads sadly: "Ah, Dominica, Dominica, such a beautiful place, such trouble."

"Well," I thought to myself, "if it is going to be another one of those times when the Creator sets me down into the middle of some earthly hell, this time I am going camping and hiking. He knows that I need a break, He wouldn't..." The people at Cornelia's Castle did not seem to want to talk about Dominica.

I put it all out of my mind and walked over a couple of hills to the Castle Harbor Casino. I was very out of shape—even worse than I thought. (There are no hills in Lake Charles for me to walk over, and I had let my climbing muscles go to zero.) The blackjack tables, all two of them that were open, were crowded. I won't touch craps or roulette, so I decided to throw away a few quarters in the slot machines while I waited for a spot at the blackjack table. It took me a while to lose three dollars, longer than I thought because the slots seemed to have a little more liberal "teaser jackpot" setting than did the slots where I used to work in Reno. I got impatient and went back over to watch the blackjack games. It was a multi-deck setup using a shoe, two-dollar minimum bet, and the surrender bet policy was in effect. All in all I figured I should just forget the whole thing until I was rich and could afford to lose. I took my complimentary $5 chip back to Cornelia's Castle as a souvenir. I slept well.

Next morning my body felt slightly better. I walked into town to check in at the American consulate, something I had been told to do by one of the RESTORE members who was an experienced world traveler. At the embassy there was a long line out into the street. It was the only line I saw in any Caribbean street. People were waiting to get into America, I guess. I thought that they were probably better off staying in Antigua. There they would have fresh fruits, peace and quiet, year-round warmth, no crime. I stood in line for a few minutes then said to myself, "What are you doing traveling the world just to get into an American line again?" I left.

I walked toward the center of the town of St. John's. The traffic became more congested; it was noisy; people had their car and shop radios on at full volume. They were all listening to some sort of political speech. It lasted the whole morning, and I began to think no one was really listening, but then I wondered why they had all those radios on if they were not listening. I found a bank and changed half of my dull green dollars into colorful Eastern Caribbean (EC) currency. I bought some postcards and stamps with pretty flowers. I wrote up a bunch and mailed them home to let people know that I was already missing them and just to prove that I really had finally left and gone to the Caribbean.

I went back into the streets and had to keep changing my direction because I kept forgetting that, in the old English colonies, they drive on the other side of the road. West Indians must think that Americans are some of the densest pedestrians in the universe. I wandered around and back to the embassy which was now closed for the day even though it was not yet noon. I quit trying to figure it out.

Walking back to Cornelia's Castle I noticed that the only negative thing I had discovered about Antigua was pollution: the oil refinery and the sewers which seemed to be at the same stage in their development as they had been in Lake Charles when I was a child, that is, the toilets flushed out into the ditches directly or perhaps through overloaded septic tanks. In those days the gutter-hugging slime and its ground-hugging vapor would cause my lungs to have to breaststroke through eddies of gaseous scum. At least in Antigua the stuff had hills to run down and therefore left town before it had time to age.

I decided to stop off at the casino on my way back to Cornelia's. The casino was on top of a hill overlooking the harbor, a very nice sight. I needed a cool drink. The thick, stinky Antiguan air at the base of the island had made my chest congestion worse, but the hilltop air was clearer. The bar was air conditioned so within a couple of hours and two colas I was feeling better. My feet were getting blistered from the hill walks and worn-out socks. I decided to invest in a cab for the rest of the way to Cornelia's. In the casino bar while I was waiting for the cab, I wrote in one of my notebooks, "Feel like I'm sweating some kind of scum. This morning's shower was helpful, but it didn't hold. I do think that it's an unusual exudate unlike any previous normal or ill sweats. Hope I make it to wherever the right place is soon."

Next day I had until 4 p.m. to wait before I would catch the plane again, time to go back to the consulate where I told them I had been advised to check in with them since they were the nearest American office to my destination. I was sent to a back room where I told the State Department man where I was going and why. He looked long and carefully at me and my passport and wished me luck in what sounded like a poorly-practiced bureaucratic courtesy tone of voice. Although I did not realize it that meeting could have changed my life, but it did not, because the man did not do his duty and help a fellow American avoid turmoil.

At the airport I had to pay an extra $16 to LIAT for overweight baggage even though Eastern had been quite sure that I wouldn't, and Prinair had accepted Eastern's conditions. While I waited for LIAT's plane to arrive late, I wandered around in the airport. I saw some posters bragging about the good old DC-3's that Seagreen (a cargo line) flew, and I even found Seagreen's main office. I could hear them laughing inside. They seemed like a jolly bunch of good fellows. Later I regretted not having gone in and introduced myself. That might have saved me from at least one of the oncoming eighteen-wheelers.

I got another soft drink and sat down near a young American-looking couple that had backpacks. I heard them talking about Dominica. That's where they were headed. The young lady left for a few minutes, and I went over and introduced myself to the young man. I admitted to him that I had overheard their conversation and that I, too, was going to Dominica. I asked whether or not they had been there before and he said no, that they had friends there and would stay a few days then go on to another island. His name was Kerry, and the young lady's was Lynn. She returned, and we talked for a few more minutes about Dominica and the rest of the Caribbean. Like the people at Cornelia's Castle, Kerry and Lynn had also heard that Dominica was beautiful but troubled.

The plane landed, and we boarded. Just as we lifted off, it began to rain. At that time I thought that it had been a long time since I had seen rain, too long. Eight days later when I would return to this same airport, I would have spent eight days straight in the rain. (Well, not quite straight, that is, it did not rain continuously for the complete two hundred hours, but it did rain at least once each day, straight, hard rain.)

The LIAT plane was an old Convair still equipped with piston engines rather than the turbine conversions that were becoming common back in the United States. LIAT lifted me off Antigua into the bubbly clouds. They were at first a puffy white but got stiffer and grayer as we flew south.

The pilot stayed near the altitude of the clouds and looking between them he eventually found Guadeloupe, a beautiful double island, French. One piece of Guadeloupe was a tall, forested mountain, mostly national park, and the other piece of Guadeloupe was almost flat, separated from the first piece by a salt river. The low island had bayous. Bayous and hills, Cajuns, maybe and rednecks, maybe; I tried to reconcile the French bayous at home with this new place's odd red roofs. Whoever they were on Guadeloupe, some people got on, and some got off.

One thing that boarded the plane was some kind of spirit that entered with a large group of black people who appeared to be shoppers taking home bags of merchandise. I sensed, for the first time in my life, a feeling of being a member of "the minority." I had never felt that feeling in Louisiana—even at such times as when riding the city bus in Lake Charles I would be the only Caucasian. Being a member of "the minority" struck me in a strange way on the Convair. Across the entire time I spent on Dominica that feeling would come and go usually without my being able to discern the trigger since I was almost always the only white person present. Sometimes I would feel like I was an other-class human, and sometimes I would not. It did not seem to be related to the kindnesses or mistreatments I experienced, it was something coming from someone else's less-than-conscious level, some kind of segregative spirit.

We reentered the clouds, and I wondered how we would find the Melville Hall Airport. I had read that it was a treacherous strip, that planes would have to dive through the clouds that hang on the mountain tops, come into a valley, set down on the asphalt, and try to get stopped before rolling off the end of the runway into the Atlantic Ocean. "In weather like this?" I thought. "In a big plane like this?" I worried. I was glad I was not the pilot. He aimed for the thickest and tallest clouds and stayed low and quiet. LIAT's Convair was being hesitant, I could sense an unwillingness in the very skeleton of the aircraft itself; it just did not want to go into that darkening mist, but I did. I really wanted to go to Dominica, right then. I kept wondering what Dominica would look like, what would be my first sight, my first impression. I wondered whether or not I would recognize anything from the maps, the pictures, and the satellite photographs I had studied. Yet, again, I could sense the guardian angels stepping back from my landing...again...

CHAPTER FOUR

―――

WELCOME TO DOMINICA

"You've got to change baby,
and every word I say is true,
You've got to change your evil ways."
Santana, California, late sixties

Dominica is a very beautiful place, undoubtedly one of the most beautiful on earth. It is like a lush tropical Yosemite adjacent to a Big Sur and Point Reyes coast. It is dark, mysterious, wonderful. Dominica is also zatzmax poverty, insane disorder, and static squalor; it is hell in the capital, Roseau, a People's Hell.

The French once burned Roseau to the ground, then gave it to the English. I had read that and wondered why. It seemed like a cruel procedure. Now I know why; I do not wonder. If I had somewhere to put the people and their few precious belongings and their loyal pets, I would do what the French did. Then I would add something: a fence or a wall or some kind of impediment to rebuilding unless I could have it rebuilt in my own way. No, it should never be rebuilt, a lesser mistake would still be a mistake. Ah, forget Roseau for a moment (if I ever can) and let's go back aboard LIAT and let me fly you in with me, fly in on aluminum wings slung forward into the past, the human past and deeply beyond the human past.

I had been able to quickly put out of my thoughts the bayous of Louisiana and Guadeloupe as the plane cut into the rain clouds. I was concentrating as hard as I could, trying to see, trying to decide whether or not there would be enough light for aerial photos. I began to understand why there are so few such photos of Dominica, and I reloaded my camera with high-speed film.

Was it a cloud or an island? What was I seeing? I had never seen such a paradox, maybe a mirage. How dark and foreboding it was for either a cloud or an island. How dark and foreboding it was for both. It was both an island and a cloud appearing merged one into the other, in darkness.

There was the Mountain of the Devil, there was the North Coast, there was the village of Calabishie, and there were the coconut trees by the millions. There were the windward beaches, "treacherous for swimming," and there were the dark vapor shrouds we would dive through, hoping not to crash into an unseen bottom.

The LIAT Convair plunged shuddering and sliding down into the darkness, like a scalpel into the unknown. Water streamed along the outside of the Plexiglas window. I could see nothing but the deepest gray I could never have imagined. I seemed to be passing weightlessly through a layer of silent, frantic fear, falling through someone's torment which was not my own except for those few moments.

The old plane broke out just under the shroud with a mountainside alongside, banked hard as it continued to drop; as it yawed and its pitch lessened, I saw for a moment ahead of us the Melville Hall runway just as the pilot began a flared landing, reversed the pitch of the props, and shoved the brakes into squall mode.

At the end of the runway we did a little do-si-do to scrub off the last of the landing momentum. That gave me a chance to see how true it was that the end of the runway, seaside, did drop off over a high cliff. I surmised that my LIAT pilot was either nuts or immune to reality, some sort of demonic being incarnate and getting his worldly thrills riding in the parasitized brain of some poor human who didn't know any better.

Whichever it was, I thanked the Creator, my dutiful-despite-restraints guardian angels, and the shivering old Convair for getting me through that terrible thin layer of dark torment in the mountain's shroud and back onto solid ground.

Adjacent to the airport I could see a white water river; I began to realize that I finally was on Dominica.

As we taxied toward the terminal, I noticed that a crash truck had been standing by with its red light spinning slowly; now, it, too, was headed for the terminal. Perhaps the pilots had also sensed the plane's premonition. The raindrops streamed off the wing—like flung sweat, the old plane moaned and stopped. Only the newcomers seemed in a hurry to disembark.

We followed a stewardess' gesture toward the customs entry, then lined up. A group of officials, including several with rifles, looked us all over for a few moments, then said, "Dominicans only, come here, form line here. Others..." and they pointed us to a certain sullen-looking official who seemed to have bad news on his mind. Most of the passengers had been Dominican. They seemed to all get processed and on their ways in about the time it took to do one or two of us "others."

Several European-looking tourists made it through our line fairly quickly. It was my turn. "Why are you here?" the man asked after studying my Louisiana passport and my face very carefully. I said nonchalantly: "Rest, relaxation, maybe a little business in a couple of weeks if all goes well."

"You have no business here," he said, and I switched on my little cranial computer and dialed it up to "full attention" because something in that man's tone of voice sounded like someone else who had once said, "You have no business here."

I replied: "It is correct that I have no business interests here yet, but I have some ideas that I intend to discuss with some people."

"What people?" he asked.

"Mrs. Honychurch, for one, head of your National Park Service," I answered.

He gave me a really penetrating look as I heard several of his fellow uniformed officials muttering suddenly. I turned to look and saw that one of them had moved his shouldered rifle into a ready position in both hands.

Then the questioning official asked me, "Do you have any firearms to declare?"

"No," I said.

In a very stern voice matched by a savage glare he said, in a subdued but commanding voice: "Where are your weapons?"

"I don't use weapons," I replied. He motioned to some subordinates who searched everything, including my person. They found zilch, no weapons.

"How long had you intended to stay?" he asked. I was getting confused, I felt like I seldom feel, like someone I was talking to was way, way ahead of me. I dialed the mental computer over to "full communication."

I said, "I had hoped to be allowed to stay for a long time; I think that there are a lot of things that I want to see and do on Dominica, starting with a couple of weeks of rest, relaxation, hiking, camping..."

"Perhaps you will be longer than two weeks, that will be up to the Commissioner of the Police, you will be talking to him about that, I am sure, if you decide to stay."

I must have looked as confused as I must have been. "Commissioner of Police?" I thought, "that is weird, very weird."

He said, "I will stamp this for a two-week stay only. Where are you staying tonight?"

I had no particular reservations I told him. I had planned to come in, look around, then decide.

"You must tell me now where you will be staying," he insisted.

"I guess the Fort Young Hotel," I guessed aloud.

"No, you will NOT be staying at the Fort Young hotel!" he said and looked at me as if he were testing my combativeness or something. I was really bewildered. I think I just turned the palms of my hands up and looked bewildered. He seemed satisfied about something anyway. "You will stay at the Anchorage; the Fort Young Hotel was blown apart by Hurricane David."

"Isn't the Anchorage very expensive?" I asked.

"It is on a par with the Fort Young, you will stay at the Anchorage. Right now you will stand over there!" He motioned me and one of the armed guards over toward where all my belongings were spread out from the search. "And don't touch anything until I tell you!" he added.

Next!" The young American couple moved forward and were soon getting hassled over a baggie full of seeds.

Kerry said, "It's just alfalfa."

Lynn said, "We sprout them, we make salads out of the sprouts. The baggage inspector was breaking open the seeds with his fingernails. He kept doing that very slowly and seemed to be looking for something microscopic. As he continued, Kerry and Lynn looked at each other incredulously.

"Open the rest, open everything," the main official said.

A big red-haired girl waiting in line looked impatient, spoiled. The inspector was ignoring everything but the seeds. Kerry and Lynn were beginning to look forlorn as they unzipped and unbagged. Big Red said, "Hey, look, can I go? These are just my medical university books, really," as she clutched a suspicious-looking box to her bosom. I recalled from my research that there was, on Dominica, one of those offshore "medical schools" for Americans who could not score high enough on the MCAT to make it into a real one at home. I thought that Big Red was a perfect model of the American traveling brat; she was truly snotty.

The baggage inspector gritted his teeth, turned toward Big Red and said, "Cut it open," as he showed her a big knife, then slowly handed it to her all the while his piercing eyes not blinking or leaving hers.

As she took the knife quietly and carefully, the lead man waved Kerry and Lynn on saying, "You two can go." They looked like they could use a joint, but, alas, all they had was alfalfa.

As the inspector went through the medical books, Big Red crossed her arms and winked at me. He searched her books and let her go. "Next," he said, motioning for the guards to bring forward the last American. After that person was cleared and sent out of the room, the main official moved over toward me and my gear. He conducted a personal search of my things, item by item, sock by sock. Finally he told me to repack everything. I reloaded all the camping gear, supplies, portable cassette tape player,and clothes that had been taken from my packs and spread all over the counter.

I got it all back into place. I hoisted my large pack onto my back and picked up the small pack and the suitcase.

"Wait a minute," the official said, "What is that patch?" pointing to the one on my daypack that said "Calcasieu Rod and Gun Club." It was shaped like Louisiana.

"It's an organization I belong to back home," I said. "I like to fish." He waited for me to say something else. "I'm on the Board of Directors; they tolerate me even though I have no gun. I do not hunt." I was on the verge of telling how much I like wild animals when he wrote something down then waved me on. He also waved on one of the riflemen to follow right behind me.

All of the "others" were making cab-sharing arrangements which was sensible since most of the available tourist or business traveler lodging was in Roseau, thirty miles away under "normal" conditions. (That night it would be more nearly fifty miles because of washouts and mudslides.) I was about to enter one of the carpools when the rifleman told me: "This is Ainsley; he will be your cab driver tonight." I looked around for others who would be assigned Ainsley and who would be sharing costs. They were not assigned. Ainsley opened the trunk of the small car, and I put in my clothes and camping equipment. I kept my daypack with me so that I could get my camera out and get a few more pictures, light permitting. I got one of the river by the airport, and then, with the sun well down behind the mountains to the west, it was too dark to get any more shots even with the 400 ASA film.

I was ready to go, but Ainsley was not. He, the rifleman, and some other officials were talking about something. Ainsley came over motioning for me to get into the front seat; we got into the cab. He started it but waited with the engine idling. A policeman got into the back seat right behind me. We roared off. I thought: "Obviously, this is not a traffic policeman." It had become very apparent to me that, today, at least, Americans were not welcome at the Melville Hall Airport, and, of all the Americans, I seemed to have drawn the most attention. It made no sense.

For the first quarter of a mile all I saw was beauty. There were coconut palms on slopes, the white water river going down into a bold, blue sea, and high, majestic mountains poking up into thick, misty clouds!

Oh, then! The beginning of despoilment: Marigot, a village of desperation. I had never seen what I then saw. I had thought that the poverty of urban ghettos in the United States could not be worse, but I was wrong. I thought that the poverty of Marigot could not be worse, but I was wrong again although I would not know that for two more hours, that two hours we spent risking our lives to get to Roseau just over the mountains and down to the sea! Ainsley drove beyond the definition of reckless, aggressive, or unsafe, and it became apparent to me that again my guardian angels were reluctantly falling, in my place, over cliffs hundreds of feet down from the "road" to the shattered rocks and blasting sea. I wanted to enjoy an immense natural wonder, but I believed that I might not see the next mile of it. Poverty and stupidity, senseless rushing past scenes set before me as a banquet, senseless risk to reach a senseless destination, senselessly missing all there was to learn and feel, all for what senseless reason? Was Ainsley mad?

He was courteous and seemed willing to try to answer every question I tried to present, but he was unwilling to see that I was negatively impressed with his driving. Was he the only driver like that I would encounter? I figured that he must be, only a novice would drive like that, only a child with a yet unbroken new toy. He wouldn't last long; neither would his toy or his passenger, but I hoped that it would not be this passenger. It was dusk.

"Now we pass through Carib Reserve, we must go this way because road is blocked, rain has washed it away." He spoke in a severely-clipped West Indian English that had begun to take on a tone of apprehension. I was surprised that the Dominican version of English was so hard to understand since my slow southern ears had had little trouble with the variety of West Indian styles I had encountered at Cornelia's Castle in Antigua. I looked out into the Carib Reserve. I had read about the Caribs. These few people were the only survivors of the last tribe of natives, all the other tribes and members of this tribe having been exterminated by civilized man. "These Caribs, they get free land." Ainsley sped indignantly through their village of Salybia at about seventy, dodging some potholes, not bothering about others or about the Caribs who were walking in and along the fifteen-foot wide road. We missed some who were too proud to move quickly out of the way; we missed them by less than a wavelength of his blistering whistle of a horn. Ainsley seemed to be driving as if he were being chased in a dream. The policeman in the back kept silent.

I saw a familiar face flare up in the misbeamed headlights. It was the Carib mayor of the picture books in his same old shirt. Our eyes met for an instant, and we agreed in that micro instant that there is insanity on Dominica, an imported insanity. The mayor's grim features flashed away, and Ainsley scattered some little goats with a thump. "Tonight they will eat goat," we thought, and I further thought about the stories that the Caribs were once cannibalistic. I wondered what had changed their appetites. I wondered if the stories were even true. I wondered who was thinking along with me about the people eating goat for supper, the mayor, the policeman, Ainsley, or the spirits of previous meals...

The road blockages forced us onto the southern part of the island, through the Morne Trois Pitons National Park, great symbol of that internationally noteworthy government policy I had read about, the keen protection of Dominica's greatest natural asset, its natural beauty and natural order. It was indeed beautiful even in the whirling darkness.

Mad, Mad, Mad and now even fearful, what was wrong with this man? One would think that there were monsters and demons and zombies standing on the roadway, but now there were no signs of animal life, just rain forest trees of many kinds, things I had seen only in science books, all very interesting when I could slow down the blur and see through the mist we were climbing into. We had cut away from the ocean cliffs, but now the road was wet. The policeman that I had almost forgotten about said something short in Dominican patois, and Ainsley stopped suddenly. The policeman got out, and off we sped again. Why did he get out in the middle of nowhere? I figured I should not even ask, perhaps there was a house or station nearby. At least he was off my back—or was he going to walk back to the microwave tower I'd noticed?

We regained our momentum; then, more recent washouts slowed Ainsley down. He seemed to become distracted, almost frantic as he would glance from his fogged windshield to the dark walls of jungle beside us to the red light that had begun to flick on the dash and then back to the fogged windshield. "The Dreads are out there," he said.

"Dreads?" I thought, trying to recall something I'd read and a little conversation I'd had with some hip RESTORE members once. I was about to ask if the Dreads were the founders of reggae lyricism or something when we came upon another cab, stopped, a broken toy. The driver seemed to be cowering in the cab; a disgusted European tried to flag us down. We kept splashing on through the rain. I said, "Is this intersection Pond Casse?"

Ainsley looked surprised but said, "Yes."

I said, "It doesn't show up on the satellite photographs; most of your island doesn't. In fact this is one of the few places on earth that we have no satellite photos of; the clouds lie between the satellite camera and the island all the time. It's almost as if the Creator doesn't want anyone to see this place from above." Ainsley slowed down. I had finally found a way to slow him down. I had shifted something somewhere, and I was safer in some ways at the expense of others. I figured I'd made a beneficial shift, that I could probably handle the new fears or suspicions I'd created (if I had), better than I could handle going over the leeward cliffs we would soon reach.

"What do you say, satellite, what is that?" I tried to explain the strange concept, and I tried to emphasize the Creator's use of protective cloud cover for whatever His reasons might be, reasons I could not figure out but that I trusted and accepted. "This is one place I had to come to in order to see it," I concluded. He began to speed up a little. I asked just before we got there: "Where is Mount Joy?"

Again, he looked surprised and slowed down. "Here it is, but guesthouse is shut down, Hurricanes David and Allen." Ainsley and everyone else on Dominica talked about David and Allen like Louisianans talked about Audrey and Betsy. Before I could ask after the old man who had written the book *Mount Joy*, we had dipped into the Layou River Valley. I said, "So, this is the Layou River Valley, eh? Very pretty."

"Yes, very pretty," he replied.

We were on the leeward side of the island. The sun had set behind the sea. I had missed the "emerald drop," but a beautiful Venus had brightened up. I could see hints of twinkles needling out from the more overhead sky.

Then we were back onto a narrow coastal highway nightmare, miles of one-lane road with shacks and pigs and putrescent piles and slime and screaming and shouting and vacant eyes and belligerent eyes, jealous eyes intolerant of my invisible pity. If I were as poor, as trapped, would all these people be my friends, I wondered. No, they did not seem friendly even to each other. (Later I would see many exceptions to that among the very old and young.) "Is that the new deep-water wharf?" I asked.

"Yes," replied Ainsley with a tone of voice that sounded almost as if he were saying also, "You knew that, how did you know all these things if you have not been here before?" Had he asked, I would have told him that I had studied but that I had already become certain that my study materials were grossly inadequate.

As we skidded into Roseau, he hit a deep pothole and winced something about having ruined a tire. I felt that that was quite probably true, but I was surprised that any of the tires had made it as far as they had. Some of the accounts I had read in preparation for my trip complained about the bad roads tearing up tires. Again I had thought big at first considering the civil engineering and road building industries that had converted the maverick Louisiana Governor Huey Long's dreams of paved roadways into reality during a time of economic depression, in a state with almost nothing but mudpaths. I had thought that if it could work in the depression-era South it should be able to work in the Caribbean. Fixing an island's entire road system would be quite a challenge, though. Returning to practical thinking and knowing the limits of my own expertise and influence, I had come up with a more limited idea. I had contacted a national tire re-treading company to see if it might be possible for them to set up a franchise on the island. The company man said that they already had a franchise there but that it was not working out and they could not get a good explanation for its failure. He asked me to check it out and report back to him implying that he stood ready to make whatever changes were appropriate. He thought there might be a place for me in the project someday.

During the crossing of the island Ainsley had seemed distracted by whatever was out in the jungle. Now, in the urban area, I was the one who had become distracted by weird and dreadful things "out there." I never have liked cities even though I managed to study in San Francisco for a few years, but I hated Roseau at first sight. The Peace Corps Volunteers would tell me later that Roseau is considered to be the "dirtiest and noisiest capital in the world," according to experienced world travelers. I was no world traveler, but I knew that Roseau was the filthiest, noisiest, and most disorderly place I had ever been in. I knew that I had never heard of such a mess. I knew that I had never seen such a social disaster, every block held nothing but tragic sights, nothing I wanted to see but nothing I could look away from even though I wanted to look away for good.

One picture book had shown a building in Roseau captioned "Past Grandeur." That night as we cut through Roseau, I saw not one glimpse of grandeur, past, present, or future. I longed for those moments of green, high above the Antillean coves; I was in the wrong place on my way to the wrong place, and I knew it.

Were there "Dreads" in the alleys of Roseau? I thought that there must be. Ainsley was whistling through intersections, reciprocally swerving with oncoming cabs, each challenging the other for an inch less proximity to the gutterways, the sewerways, open and stinking—a different stink from that of Antigua, a dietary variation maybe, or was it the extra dilution by the providential rains?

Finally we reached the concrete Anchorage Hotel, and I felt deeply grateful to the Creator for that even though as I unloaded my clothes and camping gear, I realized that it had been thoroughly soaked in Diesel fuel from some leak in the trunk. I was still grateful for the safe arrival even after Ainsley told me, "I must charge you $40 because of the extra distance, the washouts."

I remember the travel books saying that the cab fare from the airport to Roseau was US$3.50, so I figured he must mean $40 in EC, Eastern Caribbean currency which would still be too high, about... well, after all he did ruin a tire, I thought, even though that was his own fault for going too fast. I didn't react, I just gave him EC$40. He looked at it like it was the wrong color, like he wanted the green twenties instead of the purple ones. I waited for him to react. He went to the girls at the registration desk. They spoke in Patois. It sounded a lot like Cajun, but it was clipped and much more repetitive. They kept saying something about "toxics, toxics," and I thought about the toxic waste controversies I had left at home, I hoped.

I wondered, "Could they be saying that Americans were toxic?" I thought back to the *"diable"* conversation I'd tried to filter back in San Juan. My mind no longer saw only green lights, just lots of blinking red ones. I dismissed my doubts and tried to hold onto my conviction that I was doing the right thing.

Ainsley left, never knowing how significantly he had cut into the American's shot budget.

The next cut came at the registration desk. "We must charge you $53," she said.

"Well," I thought, "it could be worse, she could mean US$53."

"US," she added as she saw me getting out some more purple money.

At that moment I crisscrossed about ten thoughts, options, emotions, and the computer said "futile." I gave her a lot of my green money, accepted the key and climbed three dark, sullen flights to my room. My friend Claire would say that I was being "dour." My friend Martha would say that I was "pouting." I said to myself, "Ouch, did I get burned!" I began to wonder if I were under "house arrest" or just imagining things.

"All right," I spoke to myself, it's just a fluke, 'pay the doctor,' as my old Negro friends in the mattress factory would say when they went to the toilet. Take a shower, just relax; the worst has to be over. Think about the luxury you might as well enjoy, sheets, chairs, you are in the Caribbean, think about those palm trees, that swimming pool, that bar, that open air restaurant. What's this? The toilet won't flush? The shower won't work? Am I back in the Sunburst Motel in Oakdale, Louisiana?" I kicked away an Oakdale-sized cockroach and headed back down to the desk.

Miss and Ms. Patois chattered and giggled and pretended to ignore me, so I pretended I could wait forever without caring which seemed to spoil the fun. "Yes, may I be of assistance?" one asked.

I asked, "Is it too late for the supper that must be included in my US$53 charge?"

"No, you may go upstairs to supper."

"Thank you," I said in my stage gentleman's voice and mentioned that the plumbing in my room did not work.

Upstairs in the covered but wallless dining room overlooking the leeward sea was another set of mixed origin travelers. Three affluent-looking West Indians were speed-speaking through their food, one after another, one before another, and one during another. I doubted that any real communication was possible under those circumstances. At another table a dignified Jack Lemmon-looking character silently poured drinks for his sunburned, talkative, young Swissy. Another champ of an old character, big, grey-bearded, with twinkling blue eyes, a captain's cap, and a Tee-shirt that said "40 Foot Yacht Needs Female Crew Inquire Here," graciously and pleasantly enthralled the middle-aged Cinderella he had found. Yes, I thought, all those people can afford to leave a tip.

A waitress came. She showed me a menu with an elegant cover. Inside there was a description of supper, not a choice (except coffee or tea), just a description. I reflected. Why was she showing me this menu if this process were to be done in the style of Tujaques of New Orleans? Why not just start with the first course? She saw my crimped forehead and looked like she was sorry and wanted to explain. Suddenly my tired mind saw a possibility: For the US$53 customer there is no choice, like there would be for those with extra cash, but she, as a compassionate human being, had somehow instituted a policy device to protect the pride of the few non-millionaires Customs assigns to the Anchorage. I looked up and smiled and said quietly, "It all looks so nice, anything you suggest, but no coffee or tea, please. I'm very tired, I need to be able to sleep."

She looked like someone who has finally had an idea actually work. She smiled, too, held the menu to her chest and seemed to want to say something, then thought better of it, just smiled some more and went back to the kitchen. I felt better; I had finally been in the presence of a real back-home kind of person.

After a very bland American supper and a drink of good water, I went back to my room. The water in the pipes had been turned on. I was relieved. Then, I gave myself and my Dieseled clothes a nice long, cold shower. (I found no warm showers in the Caribbean, but I was so pleased to find any shower working that I shivered in ecstasy every time.) The surf outside put me to sleep.

CHAPTER FIVE

THROUGH ROSEAU-COLORED GLASSES

"And when I tried it, I could see you fall
And I decided, it's not a trip at all."
The Turtles, California, mid-sixties

The next morning I skipped the Continental breakfast, walked past the desk clerk who seemed to be surprised about something and picked up the phone to make a call. Outside I was lucky to find a taxi waiting for a fare. I took it into the center of Roseau.

During my research before the trip I had written to the island's Barclay's Bank asking them a few pertinent questions about the financial situation in Dominica. They had replied with encouragement and an invitation to come on down and to speak to a certain bank officer. I took the letter of encouragement and invitation into the bank. I exchanged some more green money for red and purple money and asked the teller where I would find Mr. Encouragement and Invitation. The teller said, "He is no longer on the island. You should see..." who ended up saying, "We cannot help you now; you should go to the government building and see the Minister of such and such..."

At the government building I went to see that Minister who sent me to another who said, "Go see..." At least the entire government was all in one building, like it could have been in Baton Rouge except for the redundant inefficiencies. I think that I saw or tried to see the entire "Immature Bureaucracy" as another American would label it for me a while later.

I stopped and looked at the building itself. I wanted to get my mind off the runaround. The building looked like modern Arabian, something out of Mediterranean Africa. It was white with a central stairwell that opened to the sky. The rain poured into the stairwell and blew around in a vortex showering the offices on each floor since they were simply open to the stairwell for ventilation. It would have been a topnotch design in a Syrian desert, but where it rains at least four hundred inches a year? (I found out a few days later that there was indeed a Middle Eastern influence on the island, in fact, much of the island's economy had been "enhanced" by "investment" led by a single family from Syria.)

In the rain swept atrium I saw a sign that said Secretary of Planning and Development. That sounded like someone who would have to be a conceptual thinker. It turned out that the man was exactly that and more. He was one of the freest thinkers I have ever met. His name was Erickson Watty. He was kind, brilliant, but visibly preoccupied and pensive. I was impressed by his courtesy and the efficiency of his logic. We discussed several of my ideas, and he suggested others but kept emphasizing to me: "You could not have chosen a worse time to come to Dominica." I asked why, but all he could say was, "We are under a State of Emergency, why don't you leave and return later?"

I emphasized to him that I believed in cosmic guidance, that I believed that given everything I had been involved in during my life so far, that I had probably somehow landed in Dominica just about when the Creator wanted me to, give or take a day; accordingly, I would stay. I told Secretary Watty that I could hardly believe the extreme difference that existed between the marvelous natural beauty and the horror of the human situation. I told him that I would not be surprised if the Creator had not allowed the social hell to exist on such a natural paradise simply so that the world could someday see a model restoration of human dignity and peace and harmony, all things that I thought to be inevitable since the natural system on Dominica was so overpowering and so orderly. I told him that I thought that all the elements that would be required for human survival the way the Creator envisioned it were already present on his island. Unfortunately for the people of Dominica, however, a jealous force, an evil force also considered Dominica a model, another Eden to be defiled.

Secretary Watty got up and went to his window. He looked silently out over the rotting shacks and crying people, then up toward the rain forest and the misty peaks. He said, "Yes, sometimes those of us who have lived in Roseau too long forget, sometimes we do not see what we have seen before." He turned back to me and said, "If you are bound to stay for a while, then you should go see Mrs. Honychurch at the Park Service. She is the one who wrote much of the Park Policy you spoke of, and you two will probably enjoy talking to each other." He told me how to find the Park Service building. I thanked him and then I left without telling him that I had already exchanged mail with Mrs. Honychurch telling her that I had been a Park Ranger-Naturalist in Yosemite. I had asked her if I could be one in Dominica in return for room and board. She had encouraged me to come to Dominica for an interview.

I decided to walk the streets of Roseau on the way to Mrs. Honychurch's suburban office. The small cars and minibuses were still dodging each other at the expense of pedestrians. There were no traffic lights. There were no traffic signs. There were no traffic cops. It was chaos, motorized anarchy, gasoline-fed gargoyles chasing Diesel-drinking demons. Two little girls had set up a table on the sidewalk near a dangerous intersection. They looked defeated. "Are y'all selling candy?" I asked.

They nodded "Yes." Their eyes lost some of the street urchins' vacant look.

"What kind?" I asked.

"Tamarind."

"Where have I recently heard that word, I thought—oh yes, the girl who predicted Reagan's close call, that TV psychic, was named Tama Rend, I believe. Hmm, I thought further, maybe I'd better not try this stuff after all." The vacant look was coming back into their eyes.

"What is tamarind candy made from?" I asked ignorantly.

They almost giggled, caught themselves and very courteously said, "Tamarinds," and burst into smiles as they saw that I appreciated the humor in my own foolishness and was smiling, too.

"Well," I said, "I will have to try some of this tamarind candy, how much?" It was a dime in their money, maybe just a penny; whatever it was, I realized that it was too flavorful and unique to be sold to me for that price, so I gave them some extra money and asked, "What is a tamarind, whatever it is, there are none where I grew up." They seemed sorry about that and described a fruit pod and a tree and pointed up into the mountains. I thanked them, complimented their candy, and left. Two little girls' eyes were not vacant, and it had taken so little to turn around whatever evil had stolen their hope, just a little respect and affection. Yes, I was, after all, where He had meant me to be, for some reason, if not for my own.

On the way to Mrs. Honychurch's office I saw a little park overlooking the sea to the west and the slums in the other directions. It was a lovely place with a small pavilion and no people. "Why are there no people using this little park?" I wondered. "Here it is, right next to all the squalor and tragedy. Here it is, a nice little escape spot with one of the rarest views on earth, and no one is here. A few flower children or a Cajun family could get things rolling, could show these frantic thousands and those defeated thousands how to mellow out."

I walked on, taking pictures except when people would see me raise my camera. Then, they would usually wave me off or say, "One dollar for picture," which, of course, I would not pay. (Some photographers have paid the people for past pictures, but I consider it to be a type of reverse exploitation; if a smile is not given freely, it is not a smile.) I did realize that most of the people who did not want their pictures taken were reluctant for reasons of personal pride. They were trying to guard what little dignity had not been stripped from them. In their views, my pictures of their tragedies could only have been used for purposes of value to me and possibly my selfish alter ego who would point to the misfortune of others, go tsk-tsk, and make no attempt to help. I did not photograph the many beggars, amputees, noseless syphilitics, urchins, and crying wretches that I saw in Roseau. Will I make any attempt to help? Will you? I think that we all would if we just could figure out what to do. I pray for that. I believe that we can help if we are asked, but a key problem is that things are so desperate in Roseau that the norm is selfishness, it has to be for survival. Hence, it is hard for the people there to believe that generosity and sharing are ever motivated by anything other than selfishness. Furthermore, based upon my short stay in Roseau, I came to believe that the few semi-affluent forces that do exist on Dominica tend to reinforce the cutthroat and suspicious attitudes that drive away the truly well meaning people.

Fortunately, there are government officials like Secretary Watty who should be able to improve communications among the daring and bold and good people of the earth. Unfortunately, there are other government officials, (I am sure that I need not go into detail for American readers who know that kind firsthand), who are sludge-headed, timid, personal security hung-up, and parasitic. Such people exist throughout the species. It will take cosmic intervention to halt their development, but it is up to the rest of us to surmount the barriers they create especially when they are in governing positions. I believe that it is important to render unto Caesar whatever he deserves whether it be respect or destruction. (I'll let the theologians argue about whether or not activism is a human mistake or a cosmic weapon. I have to be honest with myself and TRY to change the world for the better because if I do not, I would not be doing what I am capable of doing, I would be wasting my time on this planet. It's my choice.)

CHAPTER SIX

WHAT TROUBLE?!

"If you ever leave me, gonna make it hard to believe in you
Cause we all need each other, and I only know it's true."
The Grateful Dead, San Francisco, sixties

I found the Park Service office next to Radio Dominica. The building looked like one of the River Road Cottages near Baton Rouge. It was in good repair unlike almost every structure in Roseau, and it had been painted sometime during the past couple of years. I walked up the steps and onto the porch noticing that it was not screened and then realized that there were no mosquitoes flying around; in fact I had not been bitten once since I arrived on Dominica. "How odd, a rainy, tropical, warm place, and no mosquitoes, another asset," I thought and went on in.

"Yes, may we help you?" said the young lady sitting behind a table with a Park Ranger.

"I would like to see Mrs. Honychurch, please." They seemed stunned. They looked at each other and back at me.

"Who are you?" she asked.

"I am Michael Tritico. I am from Louisiana in the United States. I used to be a Park Ranger and a Naturalist for the U.S. Park Service," I replied sensing that something was wrong and that the sooner they felt at ease, the sooner I could quit answering their questions and get some of mine answered.

"What do you want?" she asked.

"I want to talk to Mrs. Honychurch," I said a little more quietly. I was beginning to have to fight a feeling I get sometimes when I am trying to communicate with people who cannot communicate. I was hoping that I was not in that kind of situation.

"Why do you want to talk to her?" the Park Ranger asked.

"I have read about the national policy that she helped put together, the policy for protecting and making the best use of Dominica's natural wonders. I admire that policy, and I would like to help implement it if I can. My training, education, and work experiences all these years have been in that capacity. I'm good at it, and I thought that I might be able to help."

"We cannot pay you," the young lady said.

"I would not have to be paid, I have my camping gear; if I could just get a work permit, then I could stay more than two weeks," I was nearly pleading.

"There is no way, the project is over."

Now I was stunned. How could a national park project be over? To me that was like saying, "The mountains have vanished, life is extinct." I asked, "How could the project be over?"

She said: "Hurricanes, other priorities, the government is not certain that there will be money."

I asked: "Are you Mrs. Honychurch?"

She said, "No, Mrs. Honychurch is no longer on the island."

"When will she be back?" They looked at each other and hesitated. I was beginning to let my frustrations show because I was convinced that they did not want to be talking to me even though I had not given them a reason to be reluctant; something was very wrong, and I was going to find out exactly what.

"She may not come back; no one knows."

"Where did she go?" That seemed to really bother them.

"We do not know."

"Why did she leave?" I was on the verge of anger when I saw the tension blend over into a strange type of fear.

"You know, because of the trouble," she said.

I thought about that and shook my head: "No, I don't know, what trouble?"

They began to see my honesty. "Her husband was kidnapped."

"When?"

"Not long ago."

"Is he all right?"

"No one knows."

"Then, why did she leave?" I asked. That brought on a puzzled silence. I explained: "It seems to me that if her husband were still missing, she'd be trying to help the police find him or at least be standing by waiting for a message from the kidnappers."

There was more puzzled silence, then the park ranger said, "Who sent you here?"

I wondered the same thing, but I said, "Secretary Watty." They looked at each other again.

I asked, "Why was Mr. Honychurch kidnapped?"

"No one knows." They saw my suppressed scorn for that answer; I didn't even have to say that I expected at least a speculation.

"Well, supposedly, the kidnappers said what they wanted was the release of two of their group, two of them that are being held for murder."

"What group is that?" I asked.

"The Dreads." I nodded that I had heard of them. "Why don't you go see the other Americans, they will tell you," she seemed to be almost begging me to leave.

"What other Americans?"

"The Peace Corps."

"Where are they?" I asked and she quickly described the route. By then the young American couple had wandered in, Kerry and Lynn. They looked frazzled. They looked like someone had sent them to see Mrs. Honychurch.. "Hi, Kerry, hi Lynn, how's everything?"

"Hi, Michael, it's okay. We're going up to the national park. We stopped by to get some information."

I almost laughed out of some sort of weird sense of humor that hit me for a moment, then said, "Yeah, I might go up there soon, guess I'd better get some stuff like that, too." So Kerry, Lynn, and I each bought some nature guides, and I left alone to go over to the Peace Corps who were based at the former Botanical Gardens.

On the way I ended up lost high above Roseau in a quiet suburb. Some ladies by a creek were washing clothes on rocks and old rubboards like the one my grandmother used. I talked to some of the inhabitants who were carrying things in big bundles on their heads. I wanted to ask how they could balance that stuff without using their hands, but I decided that that would be like asking how to ride a bicycle, I'd just have to try it myself sometime. One was named Star, and she had twinkles in her eyes. "I have a son named Michael," she said.

"It's my favorite name," I said, "although sometimes I wonder if that might have anything to do with me always getting into weird messes where everyone else seems to know what's going on, and yet I have to get it straightened out." She chuckled knowingly, and I felt like I might as well continue even though no one ever seemed to be able to enter that monologue, must be a rule of engagement of some kind. I continued, "It's a strong name; I think it brings extra strength for the extra problems."

She smiled a 'yes' smile. Then we discussed how Hurricane David blew some houses over a two hundred-foot cliff down into the ravine below us. She seemed momentarily surprised when I told her that I had watched David for several days before he hit the Devil's Mountains. I asked whether or not the people had had warnings during those days, had they time to board up, get supplies together, and she shook her head "No." She asked, "How did you watch David?"

"Oh, the satellite took pictures of the storm, and it was on TV; Rob Robin, our weathercaster, kept us up to date." I was, at first, again not remembering the complexities of the concepts I was introducing, but I soon realized it. I realized that I had seen no evidence of TV on Dominica, heard no weathercasts, and seen no satellites through the clouds. I sort of wanted to get into a discussion of our lunar landings with Star because she was very, very bright, but she was getting a little too skeptical.

I returned to the concept of hurricanes: "My Aunt Alice died in a hurricane in Louisiana in 1957, Hurricane Audrey." Star was very sorry. I explained how the land was flat in Louisiana, no mountains to climb up and how the sea just rolled right on inland over everything for thirty miles, drowning about six hundred people and scaring me and my grandfather. She said she was frightened, too, during David and Allen. I told her the Audrey tragedy was one reason we now had satellites and the TV warning system. I told her I hoped that the next time a hurricane was headed for Dominica, her government would warn the people much earlier. She, too. Then she showed me the right way to the Botanical Gardens.

I had read that the Gardens were a showplace at one time, one of the major attractions on Dominica because people seriously interested in the study of tropical beauty had spent many years planting and cultivating rare and representative plants from Dominica and other islands all in that one place. It became possible to study without having to run the risk of being bitten by fer de lances (there are none on Dominica) or piranhas. It was a nice idea and it worked, just as many ecological studies could work on Dominica. The withdrawal of the English subsidy system, the hurricanes, and the present chaos had left the Botanical Gardens in very poor condition. The Peace Corps had sent some volunteers to try to help restore them. They had an airy little building surrounded by a neatly trimmed hedge and a terraced lawn. Their minibus was still lying crushed under a giant tree that David had recycled.

I was very hot and sweaty even though the humidity was nothing like it is in South Louisiana (gummy, something evapotranspired from the vast but disappearing marshlands). I walked in and a Dominican lady asked me what I wanted. I asked to speak to someone from the Peace Corps. She directed me around a partition. There were a young man, a pretty young lady, and Jerry, one of my all-time favorite characters. (No, I did not know Jerry prior to the Dominica trip, but I had always known that someone like that had to exist somewhere.) Jerry was in his fifties and loved it. The pretty young lady and the young man seemed glad that Jerry loved it. They seemed like a very carefully selected crew each with his or her own special talents, and the more we talked and the more of the crew I met in the next few days, the more I became convinced that they were saints. I got that impression first from the young lady who, even though she was from up North, immediately offered me a cool glass of water. I really needed it. I took off my pack and sat down.

I explained that the park service people had sent me over and why. I said that I could not figure out what was going on, kidnappings, policemen in the back seat, no camping allowed; I was trying not to get paranoid, but I knew that something was not what it seemed on Dominica, I just was not sure what it was. Jerry made me feel slightly better by telling me that I must have a few brains anyway since I had figured that much out in less than twenty-four hours. They all laughed and so did I. It was so good to find laughs there, it restored my feeling of being on earth instead of in hell. Then they gently and kindly began the process of trying to give me a crash course in coping with culture shock, how not to make people uncomfortable, how to sort through various layers of Dominican reality. They told me what they knew about the kidnapping, the State of Emergency, and the economic situation, that it was as I thought, a very chaotic situation.

They were puzzled about some of the experiences I had had: Customs, the policeman, being sent to see Mrs. Honychurch, even being told I could not go hiking and camping because I might get kidnapped. I was very interested in hearing the Peace Corps staff's speculations. After tossing it back and forth, they agreed that things were just tense and if the government people, for some reason, did not want me to go camping, I should just forget that idea. I explained about my money situation and how camping was central to my budget plans. Jerry suggested that I check out of the Anchorage and into the Cherry Lodge where he was staying. They all assured me that I had no reason to get paranoid, that the people of Dominica were not malicious.

The young lady and the young man had to leave to go do some work. I stayed and talked with Jerry for a while. I asked for a clarification of the terms "Rasta" and "Dreads." He described a gradient type of population, a moderately significant fraction of Dominica's total population, that fraction being comprised mostly of harmless philosophers or dreamers who had professed an attachment to the teachings of Jah Rastafarian, someone from another island. "Well," I thought shallowly, "Jah is a pretty good name, too, the name of the Creator, guess I'd better hear more about this bunch of people who someone said would kidnap me if I go camping."

Jerry went on about the gradient that existed in the Rastafarian population: "At one end are people something like Flower Children and at the other end are 'The Dreads,' something like the Weathermen of the early seventies, people who did resort to violence from time to time and who were said by some to have been paid by the government to be involved in other illegal activities such as marijuana smuggling and political subversion."

I thought back to my California days and the origins of whatever Jerry was talking about, the Dreads or the Weathermen. I didn't ask because my thoughts shifted to wondering how hard it could be for anyone to subvert a government that seemed almost non-existent in the first place. I asked Jerry about the apparent anarchy in the streets, the noise, water supply problems in the midst of clean rivers, the many accidents that did seem to happen and the many more that would be happening if this were the United States and people were as reckless. He said that it did all seem inexplicable on the surface but that he, after a couple of years, was beginning to put it together, he thought. Jerry was obviously a compassionate man, just as sensitive to the tragedies surrounding us as any of the other Americans but less naïve, less frustrated, more patient but actually more willing to face what was needed in Dominica (i.e., a truly radical change in the approach to solving problems.)

One thing that might work, he suggested, would be a cessation of the multitude of international giveaways, none of which was really working on Dominica. By such a withdrawal of inefficient subsidies, there would be stimulated, firstly, and for a short time, more suffering and chaos, but secondly, a rejection of the dependent, beggardly attitude that pervades the capital, Roseau. As Roseau would bottom out (and it can't have far to go), the people's minds would again focus on the national assets of Dominica rather than those of "superior" nations. There would be a new sense of conservation of things such as forests, essential machinery, learning opportunities, families, and good will.

I asked Jerry about the potential hardships that could be caused during the initial period when aid would be withdrawn, specifically, "How could things get worse when they are already so bad?" He said that he understood what I was thinking but that he had seen another place or two worse in the western hemisphere, one in Jamaica where the "Dreads" had been first generated and another in Haiti. Fortunately for Dominica, however, there would be more of a chance to bounce off the bottom onto a firm, working platform than could be hoped for in those other places. Jerry said something about there being a better chance for change on Dominica than where the original Dreads had been faced with outright impossibilities.

I asked whether or not it might be possible for the government to just shift things laterally to that firm first step up rather than letting all gains be lost and counting on a rebound out of hell. He said something to the effect of "It's being tried, but it's obviously not working, no matter who is in charge. It can't work, not if the people are going to be both free and self-sufficient. First they must become self-sufficient, otherwise their 'benefactors' will continue to attempt to control them and the spirit of freedom will continue to rebel and this constant disorder will generate even more inefficiency, completely undoing anything any benefactors might be trying to do." I thanked Jerry and said I'd see him later, that I would go check out of the Anchorage and into the Cherry Lodge. I sensed that much of what Jerry had been trying to communicate to me had passed just over my head.

I began walking toward the Anchorage and came to a place called la Robe Creole Tavern. The similarities between the heritages of Dominica and south Louisiana kept hitting me, streets named Peveteau, villages named Dublanc, people named Benoit; I went into la Robe Creole. It was the nicest place I had seen (or would see) in Roseau. There was a beautiful woven grass mat on the floor, lots of pretty wood furniture, some lamps hanging from hooks in the ceiling—it was nice. I had pumpkin soup.

Back on the road I ran across the office of one of the newspapers I had written to and asked to send me a representative copy. This one, *The Chronicle*, had replied within a month, but the *Star* had not. (Later I found out that the *Star* had finally arrived back home, censored.) I went into the office. Several young people were busily newspapering; it looked very much like the office of the *Vieux Carre Courier*. "Hello, I would like to thank you for having sent a copy of your paper to me in Louisiana a few weeks ago. It was very nice."

The young lady came over and said, "Oh, you are welcome, thank you, which issue was it?"

I said, "The one with the anti-marijuana articles, and the story on the American doctor and his family over at Marigot."

"Oh, yes," she said. She was looking at my camera.

I said: "I'm getting a lot of interesting pictures, but the low light, the rain and clouds are making it very difficult to get sharp shots of scenery. Do y'all print postcards? I was interested in that because the few postcards that were for sale were certainly not the shots I would have taken or printed.

"No," she said.

"Well, I expect to get some postcard quality pictures when I get out into the bush. Do you think that your machines could print them if I would bring them back?"

"No," she said, "maybe some other island."

"Well, thanks again for the paper."

"You're welcome."

I perceived in that young woman an inertia of impotence, an almost instinctive resignation to what she, like many Dominicans believed to be reality, that some things just could not be done, just would not work, therefore they deserved no further attention. Her negative inertia reminded me of the contradictions at home – the busy *View Carre Courier* reformers up against their own impediments.

Next door was Tropicrafts, the convent enterprise that trains young girls to weave the grass mats like the ones I had seen in la Robe Creole. The travel books had said that visitors were welcome, and it was worth a stop. I went in. The first floor was a huge room. Tables were around its edges, but most of the space was taken up by partially finished mats laid out on the floor. Girls were sitting spread-legged by each mat weaving the kush-kush grass units together. A matronly supervisor was going over account books at a desk. She asked, "May I help you?" I walked over, and we talked for a while about the industry. She seemed a little surprised when I told her that this activity was the only one mentioned in every one of the travel books I had found about Dominica. She was pleased that the activity and the mats themselves were beginning to get an international reputation for durability.

"Yes," I said, "it looks to me like you have somehow overcome whatever seems to be holding back the rest of the people in Roseau." Again she looked pleased but gave the credit to others. I mentioned that I had some friends with a gift shop and importing business in Louisiana and that they would probably be interested in trying to resell some of the mats or wall hangings when I let them know that the quality was as good as it was. She immediately sent for two girls. One she told to go get me a "flower unit," and the other she sent to get a pamphlet with prices marked by pictures of each product. The girl came back with the "flower unit," a very strong and tightly woven pad about eight inches in diameter. I offered to pay her for it, but she insisted that I could have it to show my friends. Then, while we were waiting for the girl to come back with the price-marked pamphlet, we got into a discussion of the United States.

She, like many West Indians, was keenly tuned to current political events in the United States. Most of the West Indians are careful to remain neutral in any comments they make about U. S. politics, but sometimes it is apparent that they do have favorite United States politicians and ones that they do not care for. I was quite surprised that most West Indians I talked to were less impressed with Jimmy Carter than they were with Ronald Reagan. I had expected the opposite since almost every West Indian is black and lives in circumstances that are economically less opportune than those we have in the United States. The lady in Tropicrafts was a real booster of the same philosophy that the old Republicans preach. She was convinced that the best types of social aid programs are free enterprise based, not handouts or worthless make-work programs. She also worried about us since our American defense effort seemed to have caved in.

That puzzled me, but I told her not to worry, the American voters had been very wise. First they elected a "nice, kind" man; that didn't work, so they felt free to elect a '.....'." The girl came back with the pamphlet. The prices were very reasonable. I thanked them and resumed my trip in the streets considering the Tropicrafts' lady's clarity of thought and her odd, motherly worry about a big, wealthy country far away from her own.

I walked the road back to the hotel. Children and goats were everywhere. The boys were rolling hoops along with push sticks. My father had told me about doing that when he was a child, but I had never seen it done. It looked easy; the boys looked challenged. It looked like something I would have to try myself. The girls were just watching, vacantly. I wondered, I kept thinking that the deterioration of the spirit seemed to start much, much earlier in Dominica than it does in the United States. It seemed to be a fact that the girls had begun to be hurt earlier than the boys. That was disturbingly obvious, even though puberty could not yet possibly be a factor; it was puzzling, very puzzling. School did not seem to exist; enforced attendance certainly did not.

Rotting fruit and peels speckled the streets and gutters. Creamy sewage spun toward the sea. The syphilitic noseless men and women stepped barefoot between the pig dung just like we all did. Almost every shack proudly displayed its license to sell spirits, and almost all the other shacks had something to sell on the sill of the steps. No one was buying.

I was walking in a kind of a daze trying to process all the information of the day. After seeing several people give way to other people walking from opposite directions, I moved out of my internal focus and refocused on the things around me. The next time some people walking ahead of me crossed to the other side of the street to let a disheveled woman have a clear path toward me, I realized why: the oncoming woman looked through me with eyes far more vacant than any of the injured little girls; she actually looked like her eyes were dead. My mind flashed to the old zombie movies I had seen. Could this woman and some of the other people I had thought to be schizophrenics actually be the fabled Caribbean zombies? Was that why people crossed the street to get away from them?

From then on as I walked I sought out the eyes and found only a few living ones above the age of reason. Those living eyes were very old. I was back in hell trapped with those old eyes in a hell surrounded by fighting, screaming, babbling, or lividly silent zombies. Together we all dodged the motorized devils, it became a hectic voodoo dance in a dingy drizzle, zombies and me and pigs and goats and cars and horns and screams and children and curses and crying old people and me and zombies and defeated little girls and a few little boys diligently rolling hoops as if there were nothing else in sight.

CHAPTER SEVEN

HOW MANY CAN FIT ON ONE TIGHTROPE?

"What ya gonna do about ME?"
Quicksilver Messenger Service, San Francisco, sixties

At the Anchorage I collected my stuff and went to the bar for a cold drink and a smile, I hoped. The bar overlooked the cobbled beach, the roadstead. A couple of pals about six years old were dipping a baited hook into the cobble spaces with each wave that came up. There was no barmaid. I went down to the boys. "What are you trying to catch?" I'd surprised them. They recovered and even smiled. It seemed like such a long time since I had seen a smile, but it had been such a short time. I smiled back. "What kind of fish are you after?"

"Snake-fish, hides in rocks."

"You mean an eel?" I asked.

"No, snake-fish, moway," they insisted.

"Ah, moray," I nodded, "Are they good to eat?" They looked puzzled and resumed fishing without smiles and without saying anything to each other. I wondered how I'd blown it this time. "May I take your picture now and again when you've caught the moray?" I asked. They smiled again. I took a picture, waved, and walked back to the bar.

A trim young American businessman had fixed himself a stiff drink and was co-griping with another young American, a black professor of agriculture. They both seemed involved in anti-hunger projects. "Goddamned government, doesn't mean shit to them, you come thousands of miles to sign contracts for the food they've ordered, and they can't see you today, maybe next week."

The professor replied,"Doesn't mean a thing to them. If I don't get to see someone, anyone who I was supposed to meet, by tomorrow morning anyway, I think I'll go cool my heels in Antigua or St. Thomas."

I went behind the bar and got a cola. "What happened, your contacts get kidnapped, too?" I asked facetiously. We all commiserated for about an hour. Then the boys started yelling, and I went over and took a picture of them and their moray, six inches but mean-looking. "Do they bite?" I asked.

"Only if you put fingers near teeth." Ask a stupid question . . . I gave them some dimes. "Look, Rasta boy coming!" they said and began easing away. I found it peculiar that they seemed nervous, almost afraid of the other boy, but I instantly forgot those thoughts when I got a closer look at the Rasta boy.

He was a sturdy ten-year-old with a hairstyle I later learned was called "Dreadlocks." This would be the only time I would see that hairstyle in Roseau. The Rasta boy came along, holding a most magnificent little bamboo boat.

"Do you want to buy this boat?" he asked. I could see that it was just what I had been looking for as a gift for my sons. I knew that it would probably sell for about $30 in the US if I could find one that nice.

I said, "It's a beautiful boat. Did you make it?"

The boy proudly said, "I made some of it. I am learning from an old man; he teaches me."

I asked, "How much?"

"$30.00" he said, almost as if he had ESP.

"It's worth it, but I'll have to think about it. This place has charged me US$53 to stay one night."

"Then, why did you stay?"

"Customs told me I had to."

"Oh, you do what you want to, don't let the police fool you," the child advised with the confidence and authority of a British barrister.

We talked about the boat, and I told him I'd try to be back next day if I could to tell him yes or no. He lowered the price to $20. I told him I'd pay $25 if I bought it, and I really wanted to. Then, I mentioned that I was sure I'd be able to buy it if I could save hotel money by doing some camping as I had planned. "Why don't you?" he asked.

"Because everyone tells me the Rastas will kidnap me," I said. He looked genuinely stunned and angered but not at me. "Rastas not going to kidnap you, do not believe those people, just go camping. Rastas are nice people."

I retrieved my stuff from the room upstairs and told the clerk that I was leaving, not going to pay for another night at the US$53 price. I was tired of trying to make everyone happy; "Let them walk on a tightrope, not me," I thought.

I took a cab back downtown. The Cherry Lodge was full, so I checked into nearby Vena's Guest House needing a working bathroom. "Water is off again, but as you see, it is not our fault."

I was back to Oakdale again. I had a 7-Up and went to my room, dour, pouting, sulking. My own odor was making me wheeze. I took an asthma pill I'd bought for 15 cents in Antigua when my bags were being held in detention during my overnight stay. I'd also bought some Tedral, but I figured I'd see what side effects Caribbean asthmatics have to put up with.

My room was next to the desk and at the street intersection. As dusk approached, the noise became maddening. Cars pounding the potholes, drivers cursing, pedestrians yelling, revolutionaries proclaiming loudly, radios preaching politics at top volume, horns, whistles, screeches and slides, and sirens and distant crashes and sirens and maddening, maddening noise! I knew that I wasn't going to be able to stand much more. Then, the pill began to work.

It was dark. Some hotel girls collected in the lobby just beyond my paper thin wall. They spoke for hours of breasts, large, small, sucked and fondled, of being stretched by "big ones" and "swollen tight for eight days after." I was being tortured. Someone opened my window shutters from the street. I got up and pulled them shut again. The noise continued. The hotel girls continued. The effects of the pill continued. My chest cleared. At 10:30 the noise stopped. I went to the bar in a daze, got a grapefruit juice, took it to my room, drank half of it, and finished passing out completely.

Next morning I changed clothes after determining that there was still no running water. I was becoming constipated. I went to the patio for lunch. A cosmopolitan-looking man in his sixties came over to my table and said he would be my cab driver. "Here it is again," I thought, "now the policeman will be in the front seat pretending to be a cab driver." I motioned for him to sit down. I explained to him that I did not have much money, certainly not enough for a cab driver just to get around in Roseau since everything was within walking distance. He said he would make me a good deal, not to worry about that. I started worrying. Why would anyone bother assigning a detective to me? I wondered. He looked and acted just like the plainclothesmen I'd worked around in the District Attorney's office back in Lake Charles. He'd been to New York, Boston, Montreal, "everywhere in the United States," "got robbed in the subway," etc. His name was Jimmy, and he was the oldest cabbie on Dominica, "been driving for fifty-five years." Ah, that sounded good. Anyone alive who'd been driving more than fifty-five minutes in Dominica had to have something going for him.

"Okay, I'll be needing a cab today to try to get more things done, how much?" He quoted me a price that seemed extremely cheap, and I remembered that he was probably a policeman. I didn't care; my feet were sore, and I surmised that maybe I'd even get a clue from him about why I was getting treated differently from the other tourists. I ignored the puzzled scrutiny aimed my way by the desk clerk, one sleepy hotel girl, and a couple of hungover-looking men standing around watching me as I checked out of Vena's. I loaded my stuff into Jimmy's minibus, and we went to the Cherry Lodge which now had a room for me.

I found out that the plumbing wasn't working there, either. We drove to the post office where I mailed out some "Hold everything, folks, don't follow this leader, I'm not where I thought I'd be" cards. Then we went to the government building where Jimmy waited downstairs with the other cabbies and policemen while I tried again to get permission to do Any One of my projects. I explained that I had friends waiting back in Louisiana for me to give them the go-ahead. They had their own equipment, supplies, lots of things that they would need to get started rapidly on their different projects, each of which was environmentally sound, economically sound, socially sound, just lots of good sound ideas, equipment, men... They promised to mail me a reply someday.

I made a final stop in the government building tell Secretary Watty that Mrs. Honychurch's husband had been kidnapped and that she was "no longer on the island."

He seemed actually shocked for an instant, then said, "Oh, yes, I'm sorry; it slipped my mind." I thanked him for the advice he had given me but said, "I still plan to go camping as soon as I can get out of Roseau."

I had to buy the bamboo boat first.

Back downstairs Jimmy said he also needed to make a run by the Anchorage. When we got there, he suggested that I go into the bar and have a coke while he took care of something. The man who had been speaking with the black professor was in the bar. "Where's the agriculture man?" I asked.

"He got fed up and tried to leave. LIAT wouldn't let him on the plane, so he chartered one out of Guadeloupe. They came and got him." Then he subtly motioned towards another American, across the room, in a suit with even a necktie, looking ridiculous on a tropical island. The other American was talking to someone. Something else was up, probably Big Brother this time.

The American in the suit quickly ended his conversation, turned, came over and said, "Are you the one from Louisiana?"

I said, "Yes."

He said, "My name is Ron" something-or-another. "I'm from the U.S. Embassy in Barbados. I hear you're having some trouble. Let's talk."

"Okay." The barman brought us some drinks.

"What's the trouble?"

"I'm not really sure," I said. "I'm either getting paranoid, or someone around here doesn't like me, but that does not make sense. I haven't done anything to anyone on this island."

"I see, well, what sorts of things have been happening to you?" he asked. I described the endless admonitions against hiking and camping, the policeman in the cab from the airport, the rip-offs, being sent to speak to people "no longer on the island," the kidnapping coincidence, and the general frustration. He quietly tried to tell me to get off the island as soon as I could. I did not pick up on it at the time, but now I remember that he was behaving as if he knew something major that I did not know about and that he could not tell me about. The nearsighted armadillo was still not hearing the approaching trucks.

Between attempts to tell me that I'd simply "picked the absolute worst time in sixty years" to come to Dominica and not to go camping and hiking "because the government doesn't want you to become the next kidnapping victim, our government or theirs," Ron was asking me questions that, in retrospect, I see to have been necessary as part of his job even though he was already convinced of my lack of complicity.

I reflected upon the interrogation that I'd experienced at the Melville Hall Airport. Now I was having to go through the same set of questions, Americanized.

I told Ron that I just was not going to leave, I had waited for years for a break, I needed one, and I was going to have one, and I knew that I would not get one back in the U.S. It had taken me too long to get the money together; it might never happen again. I was going camping. He looked at my daypack, at the green Louisiana patch and said, "What is the Calcasieu Rod and Gun Club?"

"It's a fishing and hunting club, I used to be on the Board of Directors; they tolerate me even though I just fish and don't hunt." I considered how fish hooks might be considered weapons...my mind just could not put things together.

"I see," he said, "and the park service patch?"

"I used to be a Park Ranger in Glacier National Park, Montana and a Naturalist in Yosemite, California. I thought I might be useful here."

"I see, and the Animal Concern and Education Corps patch?" he asked.

"We put it all together in Calcasieu Parish, animal protectionists working together with predators to restore natural habit and the public health, people finding their proper ecological niches. What difference does any of that make?"

He then became blunt: "Well, it makes a difference. The government is more concerned over the possibility that an American would get kidnapped than they are about any long-range anything having to do with your ideas."

I became blunt back: "Well, I"ll take my chances. I'm not really worried about getting kidnapped; all I want to do for a few weeks is to try to restore my health by camping, hiking, and swimming.

He said: "I'm sorry, I'll have to advise you strongly again; don't try it."

I started to say that it sounded more like a command than advice and planned to follow that up with a question about how the State Department could intervene in someone's trip and start issuing commands.

However, right about then a sad-looking young fellow arrived. He and Ron got into a conversation about death certificates and I slipped away. I wandered down the cobbled beach looking for the Rasta boy. I couldn't find him.

Back in the bar Ron from the Barbados embassy and the sad-looking young man were talking about the collapse of the banana industry. The English company Geest was threatening to quit buying. I thought cynically: "Who could blame them if they have to go through these hassles routinely, maybe that's why they gave Dominica its independence three years ago."

Without being invited, hoping to shake loose some kind of straight talk from the man in the suit, I walked back into the conversation and said that I was very interested in the fresh fruit supply that Dominica had and that the U.S. consumers needed. I suggested that maybe a shuttle could be set up between the rice port of Lake Charles and Dominica, a swap, rice for fruit.

About then Jimmy walked in and motioned for me to come over. He whispered that the young man was the son of Honychurch, the kidnapping victim. I thought to myself that "it's a small world, but this island is too big for the number of coincidences that I'm going through."

I again reentered the conversation Ron was having, long enough to express my condolences and request that young Honychurch and I speak about the banana problem after I returned from my camping trip. He looked astounded. I waved at the embassy man, hoping that he had taken my borderline callousness during someone's grief as a lesson that the State Department should have completely leveled with me earlier when he had the chance and thereby avoided the social awkwardness I had caused. Jimmy and I left.

In the cab Jimmy said I could not go camping—"We are about to have a revolution here, it's coming, listen to what I tell you, it's coming."

Well, that was a new twist at least. I wondered who was going to revolt and why, not that there were any lack of reasons. "Look, you want to see natural beauty, I'll drive you," Jimmy said. He did. It was a nice tour, and he knew a lot, even where the original stand of Roseau cane was still standing, something that appealed to the former marine science student in me. As Jimmy put it, "Fifty-five years driving, no cabbie knows as much as Jimmy." That I believed fully. "Everybody knows Jimmy, six months old and over, everybody on Dominica knows Jimmy," and he seemed to be right. Many waved and asked him for money, and he gave it to the most needy.

I thought: "Eccentric as he is, the people know and trust him, and he knows them; he should run for office." I got Jimmy to take me back to the Cherry Lodge.

Chapter Eight

Hanging Out at the Cherry Lodge

"Well, you know, it's a shame and a pity
You were raised up in the city,
And you never learned nothin' 'bout country
ways...'bout country ways..."
Country Joe and the Fish, San Francisco, sixties

Back at the Cherry Lodge the water was off. I was assigned to "Jerry's Table" for supper. He and a West Indian guest explained the foods to me. There was dasheen, which seemed to be a cross between a potato and artichoke stalks. It tasted bland but interesting. There was "fried ripe fig," which was a very sweet banana dish, paw-paw which was something like muskmelons. There was broken rice that had a peculiar hominy or outhouse corncob odor. I left that on my plate. Jerry asked whether or not I disliked rice. I told him that I really liked Louisiana rice, it was one of my staples, but it was quite a bit more edible. He agreed saying that Dominica for some reason, must get its rice from Guyana, and Guyanan rice is not as clean. "Well," I thought, "at least now I'm sure that one of my submitted ideas, the bagged rice shipments from the Port of Lake Charles, ought to get a little official attention someday." There was a tasty meat dish (mutton or goat, I hoped, I didn't ask) with a very rich Creole gravy.

I felt guiltier than usual, eating so well knowing that my neighbors were not. I asked Jerry about the nutritional problems of the people. I had not really seen any evidences of malnutrition; in fact the people who were not maimed or obviously diseased seemed very strong and healthy physically. Jerry replied that malnutrition was not a great problem since fresh fruit and other "provisions" grew in wild abundance in the rain forest. On days when the sun would clear over the peaks, the older children would go collect food and bring it back down for their mothers to cook. There were a few small wild mammals such as agouti and manicou which helped bolster the protein supply. There was also the fish, crab, and frog supply which was a help. Chickens did not do well because there was a lack of natural food for them in the city, and Purina was out of the reach of Dominican pocketbooks. Reminded of my idea for bagged cargo from Lake Charles to include not only rice but lentils, corn, soybeans, and livestock feed, I thought: "Ah, another idea that ought to work; I hope they read them!" Jerry continued to lay the food news on me; he really knew Dominica and should write a book about it, soon, I hoped.

"The biggest dietary problem here is a lack of roughage," Jerry said.

"Quite so," said a pediatrician who walked up about then. He and Jerry were old friends. The pediatrician was from Indiana and was assigned to the hospital in Roseau. He joined us at the table but had already eaten supper. I asked whether or not he saw mostly traffic trauma cases; he said no. I was surprised, so surprised that I have forgotten just what he did see mostly, child abuse cases, I think he said. We went on to more pleasant suppertime talk, then I went upstairs, found the plumbing to be back in order, had a nice cold shower, and tried to ignore the street noise and ten thousand dog barks while I waited for the 10:30 silence. It came, and I fell asleep.

Next morning it was still raining, so I decided to hang out in the Cherry Lodge and its vicinity while giving myself time to plan a camping trip. I went to the nearby tourist bureau office and asked about maps. I had been unable to get detailed maps of Dominica in the States; in fact the best ones I had were from a French survey done in the 18th century. I had seen real topographic maps on the wall in the Peace Corps office so I knew that they did exist. At first the ladies in the tourist office brought out a series of more general maps, but I kept describing what I wanted. They went into a back room and after some patois conversation which I began to think may have been brought on by some kind of alert they were operating under, they came back and agreed to sell me the topo maps which had been meticulously done by the English and Canadians a few years previously. I took the maps back to my room and began studying them, planning my camping escape from Roseau.

After a while I went down to the lobby and into the bar for a cold drink. Kerry and Lynn came in, soaking. They looked tired but chipper. "Hi, y'all," I said. "How's everything?"

"Okay, not too bad, we're going up to Papillote and Trafalgar today, how's it going for you?" they asked.

"I don't know, better, I guess, Roseau is hell, isn't it?" They nodded. I told them that I was going to split for the hinterlands as soon as I could get organized. The lady who runs the lodge told me that I should buy foodstuffs in Roseau if I were really going "to the country." She said that it would be much cheaper. I wondered how that could be since the food in the city comes from the country.

"Welcome to Dominica," sneered Rita, one of the Peace Corps saints who came through to get a drink. She was terminating that week and was in the process of running around town tying up loose ends. I asked if she needed any help carrying her packages wherever she was going, and she sighed affirmatively. We sat and drank our soft drinks, and I asked a few "why can't such-and-such" questions.

Another one of the Peace Corps volunteers chimed in with a quasi-Caribbean "We doesn't do dat here, mon, we doesn't do dat here." The speaker was Andy. He was a boatbuilder. Andy was there trying to improve the handmade fishing fleet and also trying to forget the loss of the sail-powered freighter he had helped build up in Maine. I had read about that project and had been saddened to hear that the ship was lost in a storm. Andy was bitter about that. He had worked day and night for three years building the boat, then suffered a crushed hand while loading it, so he did not get to make the maiden voyage. He was an experienced sailor and felt that had he been on the boat during the storm, he might have been able to save it. Instead he ended up running away to Dominica. I really felt like I knew what he must be going through. His incident for the day had been that the police had commandeered two of his brand new, clean boats, stuffed them with rotting defrosted chicken parts (from Louisiana, of course—necks, of course) and hauled them out to sea to be dumped. I was almost afraid to ask whether or not one of my home state's rotten wheeler-dealers had shipped rotten chicken necks to a poor black nation. "No," said Andy, "What happened was a longer than usual power outage; they spoiled here in Roseau." He continued: "You should have seen it! While the first boatloads were being taken out to sea, the people looted the truck of the rest of the chicken necks! I tried to stop them, we all tried to stop them, but they wouldn't listen. There are probably going to be hundreds of cases of food poisoning in Roseau tonight. "We does that here." Andy was sad.

Rita and I left in a drizzle to carry the packages up to her house. Children were washing manure and blood from their feet at the corner faucet. The noise continued. We walked past a strange dark grey concrete building designed so that the windows overlapped, and one could not see out or in because of the angles. The openings among the overlaps did let the air and wails float out and around. The building stank all the way across the street.

I asked Rita what kind of place it was. Her head dropped, and she looked away, and I thought she was going to start crying. "That's where I used to work...it is where the people are put to die...There are hundreds of them, all ages and stages of dying...it is horrible...there is one faucet that works when the water is on...no other plumbing...hundreds...it is horrible."

I crossed the street and looked around one of the partitions...it WAS horrible. You probably have never looked into hell. Had you looked, you would have seen what I saw behind the façade: beings alive but dead in hope, dead in joy, dead in the body except for its suffering functions. There seemed to be a collective-consciousness: despair, grief, regret, torment, unending torment getting its head start on earth, for all of them at once. Most of them looked past me without seeing. One pair of eyes looked at me as if asking: "Have pity on me and send Lazarus to dip the tip of his finger in water and cool my tongue because I am in agony in this fire." I was too stunned to remember to pray. I abandoned them all and caught up with Rita.

Rita stopped at a neighborhood record shop to order a custom "representative local pop music tape." It sounded like a good idea and the price was right, so I ordered one, too. We continued up a hill to her house. She had been fortunate to find a place like this she said. Housing was simply not available after David, that's why Jerry was being put up at the Cherry Lodge. The house had two small rooms. She had fixed it up with posters and, like my Volunteers In Service To America friends back home, was making the most of the least kind of situation. "They're all saints," I kept thinking.

I asked her what was the roughest thing about living in the city. She said, "The night screams." I had heard them, too. I asked her to tell me about them. Again she almost started crying. "They beat their children at night; it's cultural, sport beating, I can't stand it anymore." Yes, she had been in Roseau too long and so had I. She gave me a drink of water and I left, thinking that maybe I had solved the puzzle of why so many of the young girls of Dominica seemed to have gone vacant-eyed.

I decided to walk on uphill to the Princess Margaret Hospital. I got an extremely eerie *déjà vu* sort of feeling when I got near it. I could almost feel myself lying, dying in one of the old, white railed iron beds in a seemingly endless ward. Sheets and towels were hung out on clotheslines drying in the drizzle. The windows were opened and again I noticed the lack of screens. Flies were homing in on something inside. I could almost remember that, too sick to swat them away, their maggots chewing through my gangrene...

The overall appearance was one of despair. It looked like another death hotel. One building had a new sign up, something about a mental health project financed by the local chapter of Kiwanis or Rotary, one of the international civic clubs.

I stopped and my own eyes went vacant as *déjà vu* became mixed with memories of sights I had seen on visits to Louisiana mental "pits" ten years before the "reforms" got started. I thought of another one of my ideas, one that was halfway set up before I had ever left Louisiana: some of my friends who are doctors had said that they would be glad to give a week each year, a week of their specialized treatment and training expertise to a third-world staff somewhere if I could get them set up with tickets and some recreational opportunities wherever it was, something like deep-sea fishing or sightseeing. Those doctors, most of them at least, are alumni of the "Big Charity" hospital Huey Long built for the poor in New Orleans. Still, I reflected carefully, if I were to bring them down cold, down to this situation, would they ever come back? Yes, I answered myself, most of them would, but how could I do that to friends who are already overworked and who have already "paid their dues" in many ways? I decided that the idea would stay just halfway set up until and unless I could be sure that they would also get the recreation they need, the break that I was not getting. I refocused my eyes on the people lined up for clinics and transports. I saw some foreign-looking doctors and a white nurse busily and gently trying to relieve the pain.

I wandered back downhill convinced that I should leave Roseau the next morning. That meant that I would have to walk all the way across town to the Anchorage again to get the bamboo boat and avoid Jimmy, who would be tomorrow—I was guessing—looking around for me since I wouldn't be where he'd thought I would be.

I stopped in a neighborhood ice cream shop and asked if they had "true vanilla." One of the travel books had said that Dominica's "true vanilla" ice cream was much better than artificial vanilla. The girl handed me two vanilla cones instead of one true vanilla cone. The curse of Babel had cost me another quarter.

In walked one of the two Peace Corps Volunteers named Steve. This one had a small gold earring and a beret. He was hip. He was also very kind and bright. I offered him a "true vanilla" cone, but he said that when it came to vanilla, he preferred the Baskin Robbins version, so he ordered chocolate joining the others in the shop-wide curiosity about why I had ordered two cones instead of one. They were all too courteous to ask, and I was too burned out to even start explaining. I found a wall and finished them both off. In the meantime Steve gave me a last puzzled look and went off to do a report or something.

I walked toward the Anchorage deciding this time to go by way of the beach so that I would not have to do the car-dodging dance with the zombies in the road. I was fading, and I hoped that the ocean could tide me over till I could get to the mountains. The beach was coated with trash and litter of all types except, curiously, glass. I think that there is already so much trouble from foot cuts (caused by the sharp volcanic rock still creating the island) that someone, probably some saintly old people, go along and pick the glass up from the cobblestones. The cobblestones are the primary feature of the beach at Roseau; there is very little exposed sand. The walking is not too hard, but it would be easy to turn an ankle. It was safer than the street. No glass and no sand, a silicon-free beach—my mind was shorting out on trivia.

Some kids started screaming at me: "No, no, don't cross there, poo..." I wasn't so out of it that the sewer cascade had escaped my senses. Down and around the cobbles it wiggled. I stepped across on the highest stones. The backs of the shacks were in even worse repair than were the street sides. Whole walls were still missing; bedrooms had become porches. Hogs snorkeled through the cobblestones after something. I spotted some fish traps spread out on the beach. They were of a style that I had not seen before and were well constructed. I took a picture of them and walked on. I came upon an old man next to a dugout canoe. I asked him what he called that kind of boat. He said it was a *piragua*. I told him that in Louisiana we had similar boats called pirogues. I asked him where he fished with his *piragua,* and he pointed straight out and said "the sea." I was fairly sure that was what his answer would be, but it was an awfully small boat to be fishing from in the sea. Even the Cajuns would be impressed, I thought. Now, I understood how important Andy's work could be, just a little bit bigger and these people would be a lot safer and probably get a lot more fish. Then I wondered whether or not the extra size would require a motor of some sort, and I realized that it probably would. There will probably be *piraguas* on Dominica as long as there are pirogues in Louisiana. I took a picture of the old man and his boat.

A little bit farther along the beach I found some more old people building a *piragua* and took their pictures. Near the Anchorage I found the Rasta boy and his bamboo boat. I bought it from him and told him that I was going to take his advice and ignore everyone else and leave Roseau so that I could go hiking and camping. He was pleased.

I hoped that someone someday would find a way to buy lots of his boats to send to children everywhere; they are beautiful boats; I thought that maybe I could yet be the someone. After all I did get out of Roseau the next day. It was as if the boy and the boat had changed my luck, or, to use a more likely accurate terminology, they had been the avenue for a return to me of divine blessings.

Finding the Rasta boy and getting the boat restored my momentum. I went back to the Cherry Lodge, made arrangements to hide the little boat and some of my bulky stuff in the attic, and to leave some clothes to be washed. They were still fuming of Diesel vapors from Ainsley's trunk and were unwearable because they made me wheeze. I considered whether or not I should take the bamboo boat with me and decided to hide it in the attic, too, even though I knew that that meant I would have to come back into Roseau someday. I slipped out to the store to get some supplies. I bought some expensive, slimy cheese. (One begins to compromise when faced with exorbitant prices and the need for protein. I reasoned that it might take me a day or two to reach a spot where I could fish for protein and besides, I saw no one dropping dead in the street from slimy cheese.) I bought a roll of toilet tissue just to keep up part of my morale, a box of real Ritz crackers which were only three dollars and a tin of beef from New Zealand. I was trying to keep faith in my dream of a peaceful campout on the Nature Island.

That afternoon there seemed to be even more people roaming the streets screaming revolutionary slogans. Some were wearing sombreros. They seemed to be foreigners; none of the local people wore sombreros. One of the sombrero-wearing men was mixing a lot of Spanish into his Caribbean English. He was angrily saying something about America treating Dominica like another Cuba. There was something else, like "Open your eyes like Castro did…"

Most of the local people seemed too zombied-out to be chanting slogans, but the teenaged males who were not practicing karate on each other were following along or watching the revolutionaries attentively. Every store, every car, it seemed like every window had a radio blaring out the same rhetoric at full volume. Some of it was disguised as "news," or "parliamentary debate." Endlessly, block after block, no matter where I went, propaganda, screaming, kicking, yelling, chopping, it sounded like Berkeley in 1968 but rude, and the cops thought that 1968 was rude. Along came one little boy singing and claiming loudly, "I shall rise them up, I shall rise them up, I shall rise them up!"

That night another American "supervisor" of some type checked into the Cherry Lodge. He was also assigned to "Jerry's Table." Over supper he asked me more questions like the embassy man had, and we all talked about social and economic trends. Still, if they knew, nobody told me what was really happening.

As supper ended, the "supervisor" asked me to walk over with him a few blocks to see the opening night performance of the "Fantasticks," the first stage production ever in Roseau, I think. One of the Peace Corps Volunteers had gotten that ball rolling a few years ago, but his term had expired long before it reached the stage. It did reach the stage though, and it was a very impressive performance.

I have worked in local community theatre since I was a child, and I know how hard it must have been for the director, actors, and musicians to get anything at all together in Roseau. Surprisingly, the production was smooth, the music was crisp and balanced with the fine voices, and the acting was superb. Any American audience would have been excited and entertained, especially by the West Indian flavor that so strongly reinforced the mood of the story. All the players had mastered their roles, the lines were delivered with perfect timing, clear diction, and in a very understandable West Indian accent (slow enough even for my Southern ears). Their facial expressions and gestures were richly executed without being overdone. The entire performance was a balloon of pleasurable fantasy floating but tethered to the sinking, intolerable reality. I left the "supervisor" congratulating everyone backstage. I walked back to the Cherry Lodge alone, thinking of how the VISTA volunteers in Lake Charles had only two years earlier contributed so much to the Little Theatre's timely production of Ibsen's *Enemy of the People* despite local polluters' chagrin.

That night the dogs barked citywide till dawn for no apparent reason. They seemed to be in an annunciation mode but I could not discern the message. There was no earthquake or volcanic eruption or any new total disorder; I couldn't sleep. I took another one of the Caribbean asthma pills. Before daylight I went out into the street again and encountered nobody but an old nocturnal vagabond who adamantly insisted that he was not God even though he was quite wise. He had strange things to say; he was very wise, indeed. I listened and listened. I told him that I knew that he was very, very wise, and I thanked him for sharing his wisdom with me. He got a dreamy look, like a lifetime of hell was over, someone had finally listened, and I turned and walked off figuring he was going to drop dead keeping that eternal smile. I wasn't in the mood to watch.

CORNELIA IN HER CASTLE, ANTIGUA

STREET SCENE, ROSEAU

GOVERNMENT BUILDING

OLD MAN WITH PIRAGUA

TROPICRAFT'S LADIES HARD AT WORK

ROADSTEAD BOYS WITH THEIR MOWAY EEL

RASTA BOY WITH THE LITTLE BAMBOO BOAT

THE CHERRY LODGE

PEACE CORPS HEROINES RESTING IN CHERRY LODGE

PEACE CORPS VAN SMASHED BY HURRICANE DAVID

INSIDE THE ROBE CREOLE

PART TWO

PORTSMOUTH
— AN ENTIRELY DIFFERENT
SITUATION, ALMOST —

PORTSMOUTH DISCO FROM DOUGLAS GUEST HOUSE

THE INDIAN RIVER AGUAPA BOATSMEN

LOOKING ACROSS INDIAN RIVER MAMMAGLOW ZONE, OVER
ZOMBIE MEADOW, TO MOUNTAIN OF THE IMPS

THE MANGLE TREE MICROECOSYSTEM

THREE HAPPY GIRLS FROM THE UNITED STATES

THROWING THE FRUIT OVERBOARD

PORTSMOUTH HARBOR BENTHIC SCENE

GASPAR ASHORE NEAR PORTSMOUTH

SEAGREEN'S LAST FLIGHT OUT

CHAPTER NINE

———

THE ROAD TO PORTSMOUTH

"It's a long, lonely road
And carrying the sun is a heavy load.
It's a long, lonely road
And it never ends."
Rare Earth, Detroit, sixties

I then slept a few hours, checked out and slipped out of the Cherry Lodge. By the "new bridge" I found a transport to Portsmouth. It was a Japanese minibus, crammed full of us, sweating and trying different things all of which somehow involved getting to Portsmouth cheaply. We bumped and bounced through miles of potholes and cobblestones and longing eyeballs that followed us to wherever they thought we could afford to be going. It was the same old sad-upon-vacant yearning-look that just went back to vacant as we would pass, no malice or personal jealousy, just the looks of the truly needy.

We passed a sign that said University of Dominica, Gross Anatomy section. I thought back to my days on Perdido Street, New Orleans—lost days? I had spent two years as a medical student, doing twice the same cruel, sorry, first year, fighting the shock of finding out I was in a place less of science than of sadistically-enforced memorization. Perdido Street, no more or less lost than the others, I figured, just another street on the road of life. I thought of my student job's cadavers stacked vertically in Big Charity's cellar pit, human carcasses submerged in yellow Diesel fuel to keep them from rotting, looking up at nothing with vacant eyes. I imagined that somewhere up that Dominican hill at their med school was another such pit. I had heard that in places where the power supply is more reliable than New Orleans, the medical schools have refrigerated morgues. Yes, Dominica almost certainly would have to have a corpse pit with floating forms bumping each other in the lamplight never feeling, never seeing, or do they? Perhaps Customs would give me an extension beyond the two weeks if I would volunteer to do the embalming for the med school, I thought. After all I am qualified and given the way people drive their vehicles here, I'm certain that I would have little trouble finding "donated bodies."

The transport driver stopped to pick up another passenger. She looked forlorn. The driver said something in Patois, she brightened up and thanked him with her watery eyes and a sincere smile. He let her board even though she hadn't the fare. Human beings, I was with living human beings, not cadavers or zombies. My old faults were being amplified by Roseau, and I had been only barely aware of that! But, ah! I was getting into the country. I was hearing less noise, and I was seeing less disorder and feeling more and more of the magnetic strength of the land thrusting up through the sea. I was going to be okay.

That reminded me of something I had not thought of since Vena's, my physical problems. They had disappeared, and I had not noticed or thanked the Creator. I did that and wondered, "How could three days in hell cure anything?" I thought of my little friend, Lori, who had spent months in the hell of chemotherapy and radiation therapy and still was not cured until she died. Well, maybe it wasn't the hell of Roseau that cured me. It was probably the separation from Louisiana's ruined air and water or getting a chance to eat fresh natural fruits. Certainly, certainly it could not have been the chaos and tragedy.

We climbed up and down ever dryer-looking ridges, the iguana zone, a dry strip on the leeward coast just west of where the clouds cry themselves out. I think that all the iguanas had been eaten. I wondered what land here would cost. In California these "view lots" would be selling for $100,000 per acre. A few roving goats limberly leaped from the road to the slope back down to the road behind us as we sped past. (This driver was more sensible than Ainsley and I was very glad, but he was still a little fast. I thought about those yearly news items, "Bus goes over cliff in South America, Scores Killed.") A tethered burro pretended, like the old men, to ignore us and our noise. I missed not getting to stop and talk to them. Some of the old men had to be over a hundred just out of stubbornness. They had giant rattan backpacks filled with I don't know what, charcoal, maybe.

We passed another University of Dominica sign at Mero, the Castaways Campus. It said, "Moved to Portsmouth." One of the passengers had a loud radio tuned to Radio Dominica that, for a change, instead of spewing out political garbage was playing Sosa music (interspersed with motorbiker obituaries). The news came on and the station was changed. I guess someone else was tired of Cuban flavored "facts." We heard reggae and calypso, and the driver drove up the pace. After an hour and a half and twenty hair-raising miles, we zoomed past the new campus of the University of Dominica and into the town of Portsmouth.

The driver stopped at Douglas Guest House. There was no sign. I asked, "Where is Douglas Guest House?"

"Here," he said. I paid him the six-dollar (two dollars US) fare, thanked him and went on in. I checked in and was shown to my room. Down the hall the plumbing actually worked. Again, the shower was cold, but it did work. After lying down for a short rest, I walked out onto the balcony overlooking the street. The hotel clerk asked if I would be having supper that night. She seemed hopeful that I would say "no," and I began to realize that I was probably the only guest in the house. I said, "No, thank you, probably tomorrow night, though."

It was quiet compared to Roseau, and I knew that I would like to stay there at least a couple of days and recuperate. She left and locked the downstairs door. I was finally alone, the plumbing worked, and I was out of the city. I watched the sunset over the harbor, still hoping but not seeing the "emerald drop." From the balcony I could see the island curving out to sea both to my left and to my right. The palms, the green mountains, the blue sea, the swaying sailboats anchored in the harbor, a cute little freighter, I was beginning to mellow out.

I lit a kerosene lamp and began writing. Then, it got too dark, so I stepped back out to the railing of the balcony. I saw what my sister Mary Jane had meant by "close-up stars." There were billions of extra stars over Portsmouth, billions more than I had ever seen even in Glacier Park or "over my hearse" in Yosemite. I wondered if the extra contrast between the tropical daylight and its nocturnal blackness might serve as compensation at some molecular and ecological levels for the lack of seasons. I was beginning to be able to think again as a naturalist even though I had become aware that I was not likely to have that chance officially on Dominica anytime soon.

Down the street suddenly came alight an electric-generator-powered disco, colorful as well as black lit, somehow in place, in harmony with a reality that was becoming more and more peaceful and pleasant. I had found, maybe not the perfectly correct place, but definitely the right fork in the road. I felt much better and thanked the Creator for a new sight, stars through the coconut tree canopy. I loved it, I miss it. I rested.

CHAPTER TEN

ENTER AND ALMOST EXIT: DR. BOB

"Two things I don't want to be
And zombies is both of them."
Mantan Moreland in the movie "King of the Zombies,"
Monroe, Louisiana and Hollywood, 1941

I was having a nice nap, but something woke me up, probably the increasing noise in the street. I went out on the balcony again and looked out over the crowd that was beginning to form, lining up next door to see the Chinese martial arts movie at the cinema, which, like the disco, had its own electric generator since there was apparently still no restoration of community power after the hurricanes. I heard the downstairs door open, and a new guest was brought up, shown to his room, and again the clerk left and locked the door behind her. The guest appeared to be a middle-aged American upset about something. He worked the plumbing, then came over to the balcony, and we introduced ourselves. He was Bob, a PhD consultant to the UN on some education program they had based on St. Lucia, a couple of islands to the south. On the side he was an entrepreneur. He had brought a converted trawler over from Denmark and had a crew shuttling fruit cargoes between islands.

Unfortunately, the West Indian crew had just damaged the engine in the boat barely making it into Portsmouth harbor. That was the cute little freighter I could see from the balcony. Dr. Bob had flown in to assess the problems. He had just come from doing that assessment and was not happy. Now he was going to have the crew over to the guesthouse so that he could fire them, give them partial paychecks and money for tickets back to St. Lucia. I gave him a quick synopsis of why I was in Portsmouth (trying to rest, get back into shape, look over the business or research prospects, and stretch my last dollars). He said he had some ideas on that, and we should talk again later. I then went back to my room.

Since there was no electricity in the guesthouse, it was very dark inside. After a while Bob's crew came in, and there was a noisy confrontation which continued and built for about half an hour. Even though I had begun to stop assuming that the often-arguing West Indians really meant to carry through on their frequent threats to do each other (or in this case, Bob) bodily harm, I just could not ignore the particularly intense situation that Bob was into. I understood his position, and I understood the crew's position. They understood each other but were not in agreement, nor would they ever be. As the threats became more specific against Bob, he promised to have the crew arrested. They laughed. I understood. There was no phone, the police were probably hiding from the Dreads, and Bob seemed to be out of time.

I got out of bed, popped one of my camping "light sticks," a newfangled thing that utilized chemoluminescence, held it in front of me and walked from the darkness of my room into the darkness of the dining room. I could see the stunned look on the crew's faces, even one or two that looked frightened. They had not known that someone else was in the building and they had never seen a light stick.

"What's that big noise?" I asked.

Bob said, "It sounds like a generator."

"For the cinema," said one of the crew members.

I said, "Well, it doesn't look like I'll be able to get back to sleep for a while, and it looks like you men could use some Gatorade, how about it?"

"Sounds good," said Bob. The others looked puzzled; I wondered what they were puzzled about, Gatorade or whether I was Bob's martial arts expert. By now we could hear the bones crunching (next door, in the movie, thankfully).

I went to my camp bag, got out the Gatorade mix, went to the kitchen, lit a kerosene lamp, and started mixing, waiting for the conversation in the dining room to resume. I took in the pitcher and some glasses. "There's no ice," I said, "but this stuff is isotonic, it'll hit the spot." The crew watched me and Bob sip some; after waiting to see if we had been poisoned, they drank theirs, got up, and left sullenly. Bob took some pills.

Then he lectured me on dealing with the West Indians, on his many years in the Caribbean, etc. He heard some more of my ideas and said that I should team up with a local tourist group, the Indian River Boat Rides Association. He thought that they could use my planning expertise and in return help me get an inexpensive place to stay and a visa extension. It sounded good.

Two young boys came in with grapefruits he had ordered. He gave them a long lecture on why they should not have dropped out of school. They listened politely, then said: "Dr. Bob, we know you are right, but now we are not allowed back into school." It was some sort of rule, official or unofficial, the fact is that once a child is a dropout there is no second chance. I wondered what the schools were like for those who were still attending (which had to be very few from what I had seen). I had read that Dominica had an eighty per cent literacy rate.

Bob said, "That means that 80% of the people have learned to write their own name and then read it back." That seemed to fit with what I had been seeing and hearing.

He paid the boys for the grapefruit and sent them to get the Indian River Boatsmen for me to talk to. In the meantime one of his crewmembers came back, one that had not been in on the confrontation, Gaspar. Gaspar was not getting fired because he was not responsible for the engine trouble and also because he had been taking capitalism lessons from Bob and doing well at it. He had just invested several hundred dollars that Bob had given to him for that purpose (just as Bob had for each of the other crew members). Gaspar had been the only one to do with the money what Bob had expected them to do, and Gaspar stood to make a lot of extra money if the shipment got through to St. Maarten. It was a cargo of fresh fruit and, of course, it was beginning to spoil in the heat since the boat was stranded.

Gaspar seemed to have Bob's attitude about that, a mixture of resignation but determination to get this shipment through or be ready to try again until it worked. I thought back to my gambling days and one of the cardinal rules, "Don't throw good money after bad, parlay bets when you've won some of the house's money, hold on to your own." Bob and Gaspar decided that they were going to walk on down to the disco and reggae their troubles away for the night. I said that I'd join them after I talked to the tour guides who were just coming in; the cinema was over, and they had apparently been next door.

I had expected some older men, but these were about sixteen or seventeen years old. The leader was named Magdoweel, the assistants were Martin and Alec. We talked about their business, and we talked about tourism in general; they said that they didn't get too many American tourists in Portsmouth. I told them that I thought I knew why but that the problems could be solved and maybe without any long delays. They were curious. I told them how as part of my park service training, we were made aware that most tourists cannot handle very much frustration. Tourists are trying to have a good, easy, fun time, most of them anyway. Tourists might be looking for a little excitement every now and then, but they are definitely not looking for life-threatening taxi rides. They are not looking for places where there is no plumbing, toilets that fill up, or showers that have no water. In short I told them American tourists, the great majority of them, will tour where they feel comfortable, and they will back away from where they become uncomfortable. Americans have to be "babied," I said and thought to myself that I was getting to be just like the old tourists I used to worry about when I was a Ranger. In those days I sometimes would almost begin to let my impatience show when someone on one of my nature hikes would turn into a straggler, but then I would remember my supervisors' admonitions: "Pace the hike so that the slowest tourist does not have to become overexerted, take the extra time to show everyone extra details in the ferns or rocks, take care of the tourists, that's your job."

I did take the time to explain to the Indian River boatsmen that there is another type of American tourist, one that I am proud of and that I try to be like whenever I can, and that is the explorer, the backpacking camper type. I told the young men that Dominica could be a real favorite place for those tourists, once the political problems were out of the way and some safety procedures, like we had in Glacier Park, are introduced. We agreed that I would take their boat tour the next day. Then we all headed for the disco.

There was no cover, no minimum. At the bar I got a rum and Coke, without calling it a Cuba Libre, "No use to stir up some new confusion," I told myself. I roamed out to the back where there was a canopied dance area that went down to the beach. People were bubbling up and down to a Sosa beat. There were some ultraviolet lights hung from the thatched roof but the black lights didn't have much to work on so it was very dark. Out in the middle of the boil was Bob; he was doing a white version of whatever dance was going on. His eyes were closed, and he seemed to be really relaxed. Maybe I had overreacted again, maybe he really was in no danger of ending up on the floor with a knife in his back. "Yeah, that must be it," I told myself, "overreaction, this isn't Battle Row." (Battle Row was the street in Lake Charles where my father was born to Sicilian immigrants. Ethnic groups of all sorts had learned to live together there, sort of, as they slogged their ways into the American dream.)

The music went on and on. I spotted Gaspar showing off the St. Lucia version of Sosa dancing. Over by the beach was a white couple, medical students, I figured, since they seemed to be part of the local wallpaper. The song ended for a few seconds, and Gaspar came over and asked if I would get him, Bob, and me a drink; he gave me some money, and I went for the drinks while they went back to work dancing in their trances. Back in the bar, I ran into Steve, the Peace Corps Volunteer with the earring. He was partying with two Norwegian nurses from the Portsmouth Clinic. We chatted for a few minutes till the drinks came, then I went out again. The music had changed to reggae. I didn't know the difference, but I noticed that there were more people jamming the dance area. I handed Bob and Gaspar their beers and declined their invitations for me to get out and dance, too.

The Indian River crew was over to the side having soft drinks. I asked them why more people were dancing and fewer sitting. "Reggae," they explained. I asked them to keep me informed about which song was which type of music so that I could learn the difference. Everyone was beginning to "let the good times roll" as the Cajuns say. I was thinking how well my cousin Mike Cooley's jazz fusion group Xebra would go over with this crowd. I knew that Mike's group would have to be a big hit if I could just get them to Dominica, especially since I could hear in the Portsmouth disco the African-American rhythms of Monica, Xebra's incredible bass guitarist.

Back in the bar some more med students and a professor-looking gentleman had come in. The students were trying to hustle the nurses away from Steve. They all seemed to be friends, and the nurses were loving the attention. There was a quiet desire in the eyes of most of the men in the room; those nurses were fine. I got a third Cuba Libre and boogied across the dance floor to the Indian River gang's corner. "This is still reggae," said Magdoweel as he decided to get into the middle of it. Gaspar looked like he was really getting off, and Bob was still cruising in some other world. I felt more at home than I do at home. Everyone was really getting "down and dirty," as they used to say in New Orleans' red light district, Storyville. The music stopped long enough for everyone to give a big cheer for the birthday of a local Michael Douglas; then it cranked up again. Bob paid for another round, and I began to make my way back to the guesthouse while I could. I didn't hear any dogs barking that night.

Chapter Eleven

The Indian River Aguapa Boat Ride

"I just want to celebrate
Another day of living."
Rare Earth, Detroit, early seventies

Next morning I had some Gatorade and felt better. (I seldom drink as much alcohol as I had at the disco and was fortunate not to be in worse shape.) Bob had already left to go out to his boat to try again to get it running. I put some Ektachrome 64 into the Nikonos for the river tour. I felt dull but ready for the resurrection that always comes when I manage to get myself away from "civilization" and back into ordered natural settings. Magdoweel, Martin, and Alec showed up at the guesthouse right on time. We walked across the street to the bay, then down along the sand beach to their big, sturdy, bright orange and green rowboat. There was a heavy surf caused by large ground swells so we launched the boat, all shoving it off the shore and into the surf. Magdoweel got in, rowed out beyond the breakers and then over to the banana dock where Martin, Alec, and I got in. It was a little tricky. (Although not really dangerous, the worst that could have happened would have been a warm dunking). I pointed out to the young men that many American tourists would be clumsy and reluctant to board under those conditions. I asked whether or not there might be a place along the way that would be less precarious for clumsy or faltering passengers. They said that there was but that the tourists would have to walk on down to the bridge, about a quarter of a mile. I suggested that some tourists might prefer to do just that. They said it made no difference to them.

Actually, there would be some loss of adventure involved for such tourists. The quarter of a mile traverse from the banana dock across the bay along the surf on and then inward to the mouth of the Indian River, was fun and scenic. I enjoyed the lifting and heaving of the small boat which seemed itself to enjoy riding up the slopes of the swells and sliding down into the troughs, then up again, then down. Magdoweel was a master oarsman, and I felt quite safe even though I did have a feeling of "insignificance," as Andy, the boat builder had described it, sort of a vastness-inspired humility; the power of the sea is overwhelming and in addition to humility, it inspires respect and caution.

Alec yelled in apparent panic: "Magdoweel, watch him! Watch big ground swell! Watch," and Magdoweel grinned already having begun to turn the boat to just the right angle. Its bow cut into the crest of the swell, and we slipped downhill as he began turning us again toward the mouth of the Indian River. Martin pretended not to have noticed anything. I noticed a gradient of experience and inexperience. (I had not known that a potential problem existed; Alec knew but had not realized that Magdoweel had already compensated, and I suppose that Martin's experience was between that of Alec and Magdoweel.)

I asked Alec whether or not he intended to get his own boat someday. He sadly told me that he had already had one but that it had been stolen, probably taken south toward Roseau and repainted. It had taken him many of his few years to save enough pennies to get it, and it would take him many more years to get another. He was grateful to Magdoweel and Martin for letting him go on their boat and share rowing duties and money. The Indian River Boat Rides Association stuck together like union brothers. They seemed to be the only Dominicans I had yet met who had that kind of cooperative spirit (except the people at Tropicraft). Oh, I don't know if I should say that, I suppose one could say that the

Customs, the Anchorage Hotel group, the Syrian's various businesses, the money set, that group seemed to have at least some sort of "understanding" among themselves. Somehow, though, I got different vibes from the young boatsmen, very good vibes.

We left the ocean and glided up into the river, which, because it was small compared with the rivers back home, seemed to me to be more like a bayou. I noticed a bunch of steel-hulled, ugly, motorless orange boats all tied together blocking the stream. "What are those?" I asked.

"Them be lighters, Geest banana ship come every week, bananas go to company ship on lighters," Alec said. I thought about the Louisiana ecological disasters Dominica had avoided by going the way of lighters instead of expensive and interminable taxpayer-financed dredging. No saltwater intrusion, no loss of freshwater habitat, no disappearing wetlands removed from their role as protection for the cities from hurricanes...Good for you, Dominica!

"Why are these barges allowed to block your way?" I asked as the young men struggled and scrambled to squeeze us through between two of the lighters. It seemed to be a meaningless question to them.

Then Magdoweel said: "Money, they make more money." True facts! The rich do get their way!

We got past the ugly but practical lighter boats, and I would see one of the most beautiful bayous I have ever been on. There was almost no current. Some marshy areas had typical marais-edge grasses; then there were fluted, wide-based trees although they were not cypress. There was the usual sprinkling of cranes, herons, and kingfishers just like those in Louisiana's bayous. It was very much like home in many ways and very different in other ways. We went around curves and recurves; the natural beauty was increasing with each oar stroke away from "society." The water was clear. I could finally see all the way to the bottom of a bayou. I could see fish, crawfish, crabs—a funny red and black type near the waterline and big white ones in the mangrove roots, no blue ones, no snakes, no alligators, no water hyacinths, no blue-green algae, no anaerobic stench. I prayed that Louisiana's bayous could someday be restored to clear conditions.

I asked about the snakes and alligators. "No poison snakes, a little one like this" (he made a gesture showing a length of about eight inches), "not very many."

"No cottonmouths?" I asked seeking reinforcement of what I had read. They didn't know what that was. I described it, and they were certain that there were none; they were glad, and so was I. I told them that their swamp was much safer than ours. They looked at each other with a peculiar, doubtful set of looks but said nothing. I continued: "Tourists and scientists would love to see this; back home they mainly stay out of the swamp because of the snakes, mosquitoes, and alligators." "Where are the mosquitoes?" I asked.

"Not many mosquitoes," Martin said, then asked me to tell him about alligators which they had heard of but never even seen pictures. I described an alligator as a giant aquatic iguana with big teeth. There were some "Oohs" and "Aahs!" and "Mon, we glad we have no alligators!" Then, they gleefully announced, "But we do have mamaglows!" "Here is home of mamaglows!"

We were in a transitional stretch where the river was losing its bayou-like nature and becoming lined with coconut trees and other fruit trees. There was a discernible current even though I could still see evidence of the influence of a tidal pulse. The water tasted almost entirely fresh; there might have been some brackishness to it but not much. "What are mamaglows?" I asked feeling a thrill building inside me since I was hoping that they were going to give me the same definition I had run across in an archaic old zoology book.

"Half fish and half woman!" said Martin cheerfully drawing his hand across his waist to show where the halves met. Magdoweel was smiling at me as he rowed silently. He seemed to be wondering if I would swallow any more bait.

"Oh," I said, "you mean Mermaids!" They looked like they had never heard that term. I have heard of what you are describing; I heard them called mermaids," I explained.

Alec said, "Here is where they lived."

"Are they all gone?" I asked.

"No one knows."

"Then, when was the last one seen?" I asked.

"Oh, very long time ago, some old people saw her." I said that some of my friends who are scientists think that the big animal called a manatee that still lives in Florida might be what people used to think were half fish and half woman. The young man seemed to reflexively resist that notion; they wanted to believe in mamaglows. I wanted to believe in mermaids.

"Well, I hope there are still some mamaglows here, I really do," I said.

"So do we," they said.

I thought to myself, "These young men have what it takes to be good RESTORE members, that little touch of almost ridiculous hope, that blend of love and pragmatism; maybe we can start a RESTORE chapter in Portsmouth.

We came to a rusting, bent and fallen bridge. "What is this thing doing out here?" I asked.

"The English. This was a railroad bridge, Went to plantation." I considered it the latest piece of evidence that hopes and dreams not in harmony with nature are foredoomed.

"Why did they leave it here, blocking the river?" I asked.

"We don't know. Maybe no one else wants to work up here, probably," they said. I gathered that the English had had morale problems among the work force, something which would have compounded their self-invited difficulties. When I asked about that, the boatsmen got that same, peculiar doubting look they had had when I had said their swamp was safe, but they said nothing, as if I were approaching a forbidden topic of conversation. We all scrunched down into the bottom of the boat and pulled ourselves hand-under-hand below, beneath, and beyond the broken bridge. Here, I told them, was another spot that would have to be somehow changed for the sake of the tourist business; most tourists would say, "Time to turn around."

We went around a curve and looked into a spectacular corridor walled with giant, gnarly tree roots, and canopied in a dark green. The water was rippling now, coming downstream toward us in little glints and flashes. This was no bayou. This was like no stream I had ever seen. "What kind of trees are these?" I asked.

"Mangle trees, not mango, mangle," Magdoweel said, anticipating my request for clarification.

"They are beautiful," I said.

"Yes," they said knowing that they had one of the most spectacular tourist attractions on the island. Magdoweel rowed as I snapped pictures, resetting my camera to make sure that at least one exposure would capture the magic of the living tunnel. It could not happen, and I knew that, but I tried. I wished that thousands, millions of people could slide silently up into that motherly tube, that all together we could swim alongside each other, pulling against gravity, against the slippery floor of the constricting funnel; I was being thrust toward somewhere I could not yet know, and I was being drawn up into that somewhere by forces I had forgotten. I wanted to be the FIRST ONE IN!

Suddenly ahead there was an orifice, the tube opened up against some fingers of rocky, bare earth, and the stream began climbing up a steep, lush hill. The bayou had become a whitewater stream. Magdoweel grounded the boat, and we got out. We pulled the boat up onto the bank to keep the current from taking it away. "Here is where we want to build our aguapa," Magdoweel said.

"What is an aguapa?" I asked. "A little jungle hut. We would bring tourists to aguapa, sell them fresh mangoes, paw-paws, jellies. Tourists could rest, then we go back."

I said: "That sounds like a very nice idea; what kind of jellies would you have?" They then explained to me that "jelly" is a local term for a fresh green coconut. A "jelly" has a refreshing juice in it and a tasty gelatinous layer whereas a ripe brown coconut was much less of a delicacy even though they were okay for just nibbling. We nibbled on a ripe brown one like Americans do. I noticed what looked like a rarely used trail headed upstream. I suggested that we hike up the trail aways so that I could see some more and get some extra pictures. They got that weird look again and seemed to be communicating with each other silently debating with their eyes and fidgets. Magdoweel said, "Okay, for short distance only."

The trail was very narrow, rocky and tangled with vines and branches. It followed the stream uphill. The trees, the birds, the occasional sight of cloud-covered mountains ahead of me, all were indescribably beautiful, and I was ready to go for that long camping trip I needed so thoroughly. It was peaceful and quiet except for an occasional chirp or whistle and for the white sounds of the white water.

"Guava here, try this," Magdoweel said as he handed me something strong and good. As we climbed uphill, I was again reminded of Yosemite. The trails there were a little wider and easier to walk; its air was cooler, but the mists and rainbows felt the same. Its trees and their fragrances were of a different tribe, but their Creator was the same.

We came upon a clearing, a small meadow. Alec and Martin stopped behind Magdoweel when he stopped. They all seemed to be looking around for something. They said nothing. I said, "This is a pretty place."

Magdoweel said, "This is a place of jzhombies."

"Did you say zombies?"

"Jzhombies."

"Do you mean 'the walking dead'?" I asked, getting a thrill similar to the one I got from the "mamaglows."

"Yes, the dead who walk, here is where they walk at night. I was shaking my head and telling myself that these young men either had an incredible sense of tourism or that they actually believed this nonsense. I asked, "Have you seen them?"

Magdoweel said, "No, but some of the people have."

"When?" I asked.

"It's been a long time, like with the mamaglows, the noise of the road: the machines, it drives them away, mostly." Magdoweel, strong leader, man of exceptional intelligence was standing there telling me that zombies were up on that mountain somewhere, and he seemed to really believe it, nearly believe it, anyway. Alec and Martin did believe it. I could hardly believe that they did, but their rigidity was not contrived, their paranoid glancing, their sweat, their silence, all were real, they were afraid and fighting not to be.

Now I began to understand those strange looks they had been giving each other. I began to understand why the major peaks of Dominica were named after the Devil. I began to understand why the people bunched up in Roseau. I finally began to understand the great depth of Dominica's Darkness.

Martin got out his herbal asthma medicine, and we all smoked some. The zombie meadow became even more surreal. I continued to probe into the legend, having to balance their superstitions with my science using our common appreciation of Nature as an axis, a security device to keep them talking. I probed the illusions of Hades' Magician, that is, the devil. I resented his egotistical deceptions. I resented his unfair exploitation of the human innocence. I loved him for making it possible to show what humans could figure out and what they could and would do to overcome deceit. I loved my enemy for failing to overcome mankind.

We stopped talking for a while. Finally, I said, "Man, man, man, y'all have here something that people from all over the world would like to come and see. Y'all have answers for scientists, solutions for world leaders, y'all have something the American tourist family would eat alive!"

Magdoweel turned and looked at me. Martin extinguished the asthma medicine. Alex peed on the bushes. Magdoweel said, "It's time to go back." Alec and Martin led the way. I kept talking about the tourists who would love to come out here, not just in the daytime, but at night to try to see the zombies. The first time I said that there was just a withdrawn silence. They just kept on going, plodding through the bushes.

The next time I said it, Alec said, "We don't come here at night, no river tours at night."

I asked, "Have you ever been here at night?"

Martin said, "never." Magdoweel seemed to be considering the thought.

I said, "Well, I used to do research in the swamps of Louisiana, night research; it's a whole different world at night." They all grunted agreement with that. "It's a beautiful world at night, but I had a hard time getting helpers for my night research in Louisana because people were timid, worried about mosquitoes, snakes, loup garous, but..."

"Loup garous! You have loup garous, too? Sometimes we have loup garous here, too!" they explained. I thought so. The Creole folklore was just as entrenched here as it was in the voodoo-limited neighborhoods of New

Orleans. If it were not such a fear-mongering reality, it could be considered just a quaint historical episode.

"Loup garous and lots of other bullshit in Louisiana. I spent many nights alone out in the swamp, more than anyone else I know. I never saw one loup garou! Just lots of pretty things that no one else got to see. Sure, it was mysterious, but that was one of the special things that made everything so pretty. You could have the same kind of 'magical mystery tour' here, and it would be fun and pleasant and everyone would love it."

Magdoweel said, "You really think people would pay money to come on the river trip at night?" Alec and Martin moaned knowing that they might be about to get into a whole new adventure with Magdoweel, one that they did not look forward to but since he was their leader, one that they would be bound to follow.

"I know they will pay you money; I'll be the first," I declared.

"Hmm," said Magdoweel, and there were more moans from Martin and Alec.

"How about tonight?" I asked.

"Oh, no, can't be tonight," Alec spurted.

"Why not?" I asked. He appeared agitated and couldn't think of a reason.

"No moon!" said Martin.

"Not tonight, no moon, can't see way to go!" agreed Alec.

Magdoweel said, "Maybe."

I said, "Okay, maybe sounds good. "There were some more moans from Alec and Martin.

We arrived back at the boat. I waded out into the current and took some more photographs of the "mangle tunnel" from the upper end. They launched the boat and we climbed back in. Back in the mamaglow zone we stopped, and Martin climbed a jelly tree and kicked some down for us. Then we rowed down some more and borrowed a "cutlass" (machete) from some hard-worked field children that had come to the river to cool off. Martin carefully sliced away the coconut's green husk to the point where all we had to do to get the drink was poke a finger through and make a little hole. That way the milk wouldn't spill out in the boat, and we could have drinks all the way back. We shared with the field children, and then they went back to work wearily clearing brush for someone.

Near the sea again I noticed off to the side of the river, a Louisiana type marais, a tidal marsh stream lined with small mangroves on the mud flats, but there were none of the marsh grasses I was accustomed to seeing. At my request we turned and went up into the cloacal marais for a short distance. The water was murky. We got mired. "Quicksand!" said Alec who was now the oarsman. He dug the oars in, and we rocked the boat to get it loose. This mud did have the rotten egg odor of hydrogen sulfide.

"Brimstone," said Magdoweel, "brimstone quicksand, fuel water, hotter than river, comes from volcano." I couldn't really feel any difference in temperature, but I asked if there were hot springs upstream and they said, "Yes, very hot, comes out of Morne Diablotins," the mountain of the imps.

I considered the near proximities of heaven and hell with us sandwiched right in between. I could smell the fires of Gehenna beneath me, and I could see the celestial magnificence above me. With me in my thin dimension were beauties, marvelous creations but threatened, suffering creations.

"Hmm," I said, "maybe I'll hike up there tomorrow." Martin snickered sadly and muttered something about the zombies already having us all up there by tomorrow.

Alec said, "Bad trail, not used much." Alec was getting tired because of the difficulty of getting turned around in the shallow water lying above the "quicksand." He said: "Hey, you fellas, this vex me too much, move around boat," so we shifted our weights around and back and finally got the boat back into a more watery part of the marais.

Martin picked at Alec, "When I captain, no tourist stuck in quicksand."

Alec retorted, "When you captain, no tourist stay in boat." We all laughed.

Back near the banana barges we got hung up on a chain Geest had stretched across the river. The tide had gone down a little, and again we had to rock the boat and struggle to be delivered freely and out through the mouth of the river to the open sea. I repeated my recommendation that these "inconveniences" should be eliminated because it would hurt their tourist business to not do so, many tourists would be more likely to feel a sense of danger from a potential dunking than they would feel a sense of adventure.

At the dock I asked Magdoweel when he would know about the possible night tour. He said that he would come by later in the afternoon. In the guesthouse I found Bob and Gaspar discussing the futility of the engine repair effort. They were deciding to start jettisoning the spoiling cargo. The rest of the crew was still hanging around town which seemed to be making Bob and Gaspar nervous. I suggested that they take the river tour to get their minds off things for a while. They said that they didn't have time today. Bob said that he was going to get the Aguapa crew to help guard the boat. I said that we might be going on a night tour early in the evening and asked if that would conflict. "No, just meet us afterwards at the disco. I didn't know they had night tours."

I said, "This will be a first, why don't y'all join? It's a zombie hunt." Gaspar almost fainted.

Bob laughed, "I knew you would help those young men with their business, but that's pretty fast work, Mike!"

"Yeah, if I could just get some more tourists to go along, I think they'd be convinced."

Gaspar sighed, resigned to my foolish disbelief and my probable fate. He said, "All right, maybe. I'll have to see how things go this afternoon."

Chapter Twelve

Three Young Ladies from America Hunting Zombies at Night

"Hello, who's your daddy?
Is he rich like me?...
It's the time of the season...to live!"
The Zombies, England, mid-sixties

I went to my room and took a short nap. When I returned to the dining room, three attractive backpacking American girls were checking into the guesthouse. "Yes, we will have supper tonight, mountain chicken. I've been dying to try it."

The hostess turned my way. I realized that I might know a secret best kept to myself about the mountain chicken. I said, "I'd like the mountain chicken and also a fruit salad plate, thanks."

One of the girls said, "I'm Cheryl, this is Rhonda, and she's another Cheryl."

"I'm Michael."

"Weren't you just leaving the Cherry Lodge when we were going in for a shower?" one of the Cheryls asked.

"I guess so, sorry I missed it."

They snickered one of those, "Oh, wow does he ever think he's funny" snickers, and I realized again that I'd never be a comedian.

"Did the shower work when you were there?" I asked, trying to change the thought if not the subject.

"Yes, it was nice." Rhonda said, "You're the one from Louisiana, aren't you?"

I guessed that Jerry had told them. "Yes," I said, "Where are you all from?"

"Well, I'm from Florida, and she's from Miami, and she's from Washington, D.C."

"What do y'all do?"

"We're working women!" they said proudly (or was it "career" women—I was sort of distracted at the time, they were cute).

"What kind of things do you do?" I asked, knowing that I was supposed to. Each described her work, and they were correct to be proud, and I was proud of them, too, by the time that they finished.

"Well, we will see you at supper, right now we have to go get cleaned up and work on a song for our Rasta friends, they've really been taking care of us in the bush."

"You've been in the bush with the Rastas?" I asked, jealously adding that I wanted to go hiking and camping but was forbidden to because the Rastas would kidnap me.

"Oh, don't believe that! They are very nice people, very nice."

"Well, maybe it's just because you are girls," I questioned.

"Well, maybe," said one with a beam in her eye.

"Oh, no," said another. "They were nice to us ALL, I mean they couldn't have been any nicer!"

The third one quickly said, "And they even built us each a bed and put all their clothes on them to make mattresses."

"Hmm," I said trying to visualize that and the next scene. "Must have been very exciting for you being in the bush with primitive men."

"Oh, they weren't primitive at all! They were *very* sophisticated," and she looked at me like I should hope that I might be that sophisticated someday if I were ever so lucky. She reminded me of several of my ladyfriends back home. I kept quiet.

"We bought them this guitar. They just had one; they shared it, but it was old and broken."

Another one said, "We used almost all our money for it, but that's okay since we saved that money in the first place by staying with them instead of in hotels. They let us stay free."

"That's a very nice gesture," I said. "You are very nice young ladies, "I'm sure they'll really be happy to get the guitar."

"Yes, they will be, and so are we!" and they danced and bounced gleefully off to their room and started singing their new song. It was sort of a reggae girlscout chant, unique but, well, let me just leave it at "unique."

They each came out, went down to the shower and back, and I decided that I would see if I could get them to join the zombie hunt tonight before Bob came back and talked them into the disco. He came back, very disconsolate, went to his room, then to the shower, then back to his room. (As long as the Douglas family kept that shower working, they would have one of the most reliable tourist attractions on Dominica.)

Suppertime came and the girls, Bob, Gaspar, and I sat down together and lit the kerosene lamp. Bob seemed perked up by the new faces. When the food was brought out, one Cheryl said she wouldn't eat the mountain chicken because it looked like "dead frog." The secret had to be revealed. I told her that that's exactly what it was.

Rhonda decided that she was a vegetarian. I gave Rhonda and the first Cheryl my fruit salad plate to munch on while the hostess went back to prepare another one for us all to share. The other Cheryl, Bob, Gaspar, and I began eating our delicious mountain chicken. It was far tastier than Louisiana's delicacy, fried frog legs, far more delicious, basted in a kind of roux, no filé though, that's all it needed, just a pinch.

About then Magdoweel and his men came in. I asked them to sit down and have some supper; there was plenty of extra mountain chicken. They declined nervously. "Well, Magdoweel, looks like a good dark night, just right for the zombie hunt, eh?"

"Zombie hunt?!?" The three girls screamed gleefully. I winked at Magdoweel, and he smiled. Gaspar, Alec, and Martin moaned in harmony.

Bob chuckled. "Michael, are you really going on a zombie hunt?" asked one Cheryl suspiciously.

"That's up to Magdoweel, he's the captain," I said.

Magdoweel said, "Well, we need more people, we need a full boat."

"How much would it cost?" they asked.

"Ten dollars each," he said.

"EC Dollars?" they asked hesitantly.

"Yes," said Magdoweel realizing that they must be on a limited budget to be asking such a question.

"Oh, yes, oh yes, let's do it! Can you take us all?"

Magdoweel smiled, "Yes, be ready in one hour, we'll come back." Alec and Martin moaned all the way out and when they got into the street below, there was soon a Patois uproar that spread at least three blocks away.

"Oh, how exciting, Michael, have you ever been on the zombie hunt before?" Rhonda asked. Bob started laughing, and Gaspar got up and left.

"Well, actually, I think I'd better level with you girls. We are going to be the first people in history to go on the Aguapa zombie tour, the absolute first."

There were a few moments of silence, and the bold Cheryl said, "Oh, it will be exciting, the very first time! It's always so thrilling to do it first!"

"That's the way I feel about it," I said with other things on my mind, I thought.

Bob said, "Well, what if you really find some zombies?"

"Yeah," said Rhonda and the other Cheryl, "What if?"

"Well, I said, "that will be even another layer of firsts, won't it?" The bold Cheryl and I smiled at each other. We knew that we were in for a wondrous hunt.

An hour later the Indian River Aguapa crew met Rhonda, the two Cheryls, and me at the guesthouse. Bob and Gaspar had decided not to go. There was hardly enough light for us to see each other's faces, especially the black ones. Martin and Alec tried one final time to dissuade their leader and their customers from going to look for the zombies. "No moon tonight, very dark." "Only starlight."

Rhonda said, "Oh, does that mean we won't see zombies, do they just come out on the full moon like werewolves?"

Magdoweel said, "No one knows, we go, this way, please."

We walked giggledly across the street to the dock. Magdoweel had already made some improvements in the embarkation facilities and had somewhere borrowed a much larger rowboat. The girls climbed in. "This one's larger than the one we had today," I noted.

"Yes, old fisherman let us borrow, more comfort for girls."

"Thank you," said one Cheryl for the others who nodded wondering how primitive and small must have been the other boat.

"Well, I really liked your boat's bright colors, Magdoweel, but at night, they wouldn't show up anyway," I said.

"No, mon, but soon you see the 'night colors.'"

"Oh, what are 'night colors'?" asked Cheryl Two. I was puzzled, too.

"See!" said Magdoweel pointing to a burst of phosphorescent green as he splashed the first oar down into the sea.

"Oh, how beautiful!" someone said, and we all thought the same as he mounted the other oar in its bracket, then splashed it into the water.

Alec and Martin shoved us off from the dock, and we watched in quiet appreciation as each oarstroke triggered the brilliant green display in the sea. I put my hand over the side of the boat into the water. Green bubbles lit up and streamed away. An eerie halo of fluorescent green gloved my hand and as I opened it slowly, green stars fell from my fingertips.

As Magdoweel rowed silently through the ground swells toward the mouth of the Indian River, Rhonda, the two Cheryls, and I saw that we had already gotten more than our ten dollars worth; we had seen a rare and priceless phenomenon, one that we could lock away for all times in our mental treasure chests, and yet one that we could share with all our friends. How nice it would be if all people on earth could see green stars falling from their fingertips just once in their lives!

We entered the river and began talking again. Martin gave the facts on the Geest banana lighters which were still a problem especially in the wider boat, but with a higher tide we seemed to clear the chain more easily at least.

Alec gave them the mamaglow story, and the girls were thrilled. "Mamaglows, the real home of the original mermaids, can you believe it?" cheerily asked the bold Cheryl.

"I'm not sure," I said, "maybe they were just manatees," knowing what would happen.

"They ARE just MERMAIDS!" the girls insisted, and Magdoweel's white teeth lit up in a smile as his crew began to see how superstition gets built. I sensed that Alec and Martin were losing their fear of zombies just as surely as the girls were yearning to see a real mermaid, but, alas, the mamaglows were being coy that night or maybe they were just shy; we didn't see any, not even one.

A large school of mullet surfaced and splashed suddenly out from under the boat. "Was it a mermaid?" I asked. "No, I guess it's just a school of mullet," I sighed as I answered my own question. The girls sighed with me.

We left the mamaglow zone and slid into the dark tunnel of mangle trees. The roots were twisted and tangled like trolls' faces encapsulating our boat and scowling at our presence. The stars retreated behind palm frond shields, and bats flew up and down the corridor between our heads and the dark jungle canopy. Lizard whistles pierced our ears. The zombie fear returned.

As Magdoweel pulled against the increasing current, Rhonda and the meek Cheryl leaned quietly into each other, almost unconsciously, almost imperceptibly. The bats flew nearer. The jungle closed in toward us, the stream narrowed, the boat crunched to a stop. We had arrived at the hut site. Martin said somewhat shakily: "Here is where we were going to put aguapa, fruit hut."

"Were?" asked the bold Cheryl.

"Before zombies got us," said Alec in a foreboding whisper.

Magdoweel said, "Now we walk where zombies walk, the Zombie footpath to Zombie meadow. Do not get separated; stay close to me, I lead."

Rhonda produced a small flashlight. It seemed to amplify the tomb-like darkness that scurried in behind the beam, no matter which way she moved it. The meek Cheryl said: "Are you telling the truth about no one ever coming to this meadow before at night?"

"No one but jzhombiees," said Magdoweel in what seemed like an almost threatening tone of voice, and he turned his face back into the night and grinned menacingly at the three girls; his ivory teeth and eyeballs seeming to float freely in the distorted darkness of the jungle. Then, he swiftly turned and began striding powerfully along the trail ahead.

"Wait," begged Rhonda, "we cannot keep up."

"Wait, wait," said the meek Cheryl, and we all tried to go faster but got in each other's way scrambling to also stay in the cocoon spun by Rhonda's flashlight.

Suddenly there was a horrid shriek and ten huge black fingers flew from the jungle darkness into Rhonda's face and heart. She screamed, and Cheryl screamed, and they grabbed each other and waited for...After a microsecond of infinite depth, they opened their eyes and breathed again, and Magdoweel laughed. "I knew he was going to do that, I just knew it," said the bold Cheryl, and we all laughed, and I think that I heard some muttered references to bodily functions by the young ladies and the crew. I felt the same way.

The slow hike up the zombie footpath resumed. Except for properly sounding heart sounds, we were all trying to move ahead as silently as possible. Part of that was just the trying to get our breaths back, but part of it was an inverse effect of Magdoweel's sense of humor, that is, the Americans had all begun to realize that when he wants to be, Man can become the Master of Fear. We can build it, illusion by illusion, into an animal more fearsome than a circus cat. Man can make the cat jump through flaming hoops, and Man can send it back to its cage. The fear that Magdoweel had created in our hearts was sent to its cage almost immediately by our certain minds. The fear that troubles the people of Dominica is one they cannot cage with uncertain minds.

We reached the clearing. It was decidedly more mysterious in the darkness. Half the stars were missing, hidden by Morne Diablotins. Another quarter were hidden by its misty shroud. By quarter starlight we watched the meadow. Light breezes would twist distant leaves, and we would focus there looking for shadowy forms we did not really want to see. Rhonda put out the torch. She and Cheryl stood very close to each other; then, their garments touched. Neither withdrew. Rhonda leaned slowly toward Cheryl who then leaned firmly into her. In the nearly absolute darkness, I sensed but I could not see their hands find and grasp and grip and hold. I sensed bodies pressing together for comfort. Which bodies... pressing...

We waited, our eyes did not adjust, the darkness was suffocating. Our eyes would sweep the clearing, probe holes in the jungle wall, scan the whispering tree crowns, spin through the mist but always our eyes would search back to the stars, for light, for reassurance. Eventually I said, "No zombies tonight, I guess, not that 'time of the season' after all."

"Too bad," said the bold Cheryl, "but it's still fun to be on the first zombie hunt, isn't it? 'Shows us what we need to live,' eh?" She had remembered the same lyrics I had; she was on nearly the same wavelength.

"Maybe they are hiding on the other side of meadow," postulated Magdoweel with an informative tone of voice. "Shall we hunt?"

"No! That's quite all right!" said Rhonda as she turned her flashlight back on.

"Right, we really can't stay out too late tonight," said the meek Cheryl. The flashlight illuminated Alec's and Martin's first smiles in hours.

"Okay," said Magdoweel, and we all turned and walked down the trail. He took the lead. We spread out a little bit and resumed our quiet individual reflections. The eight-inch bats started flying a slalom course marked by our heads as if we had invented a new intra-species game.

I was last in line. I was drifting in a fantasy world. I lost the image suddenly when I realized I was being followed. For a few moments I wondered if some coconut gatherer had gotten lost then decided to follow us back into the village. Then, I thought I heard several more beings behind me, then moving off to my right, then brushily moving around to fall in again behind me. I looked back and saw Magdoweel grinning again and putting his finger across his lips and signaling me not to say anything.

I realized that he had led us into a wide human circle around a dense thicket. He was loving every second of it. We kept going around the thicket for a while. Then Cheryl said, "Hey, what's going on here, we just passed this same...Why Magdoweel! You rascal! You've fooled us again," and we all started laughing and promising ourselves that we would have to get this outrageous Magdoweel back.

How fun it was to be automatically and completely transported back to our junior high school days by a master psychologist and born tour guide! We lived again the fresh and innocent moments of nocturnal discovery and pal-side humor. We were cosmicly thankful.

Back at the dock a somber group of parents and their neighbors had gathered to murmur about the probable fate of the three foolish young men and those typically-stupid Americans. The townspeople were certain we would be the latest reinforcement of the old legends. We could see them weaving and moping between the white star canopy and the green star carpet. Some were quietly moaning. Then they saw us coming; we waved and laughed. They cheered! Magdoweel, Martin, and Alec landed as the new heroes of Portsmouth!

After an appropriate celebration at the disco the girls and I went up to bed in the guesthouse.

We fell asleep joyously and I dreamed that...

Chapter Thirteen

Resurrection of the Real King of the Zombies

"Take it from me, I know
Undeveloped mind don't mean a thing.
We got to wake up baby.
Nothing comes to a sleeper but a dream."
Lowell Fulsom, Shreveport, mid-fifties

...I was going to stay on the island and therefore needed to try to find a house to rent. I went with the child Galen who said he knew the way to a very pretty place. He said it was a solitary cabin high on a foothill named Upper Sheol. A small stream came down from a plateau and the green of the trees calmed and quieted my mind and heart, and I wanted more sleep. It would cost me thirty dollars per month, US—the house, its wild garden that covered thousands of acres, its view of the western sea. I would be able to sleep. I told Galen that I liked it but that I would have to give a final answer in the morning.

I then walked down to the ocean, stopped, stripped, and swam. I could see zebra fish and crimson darters and twirling anemones amongst the fire coral. The sea carried my submissive body back to the coconut trees. I dressed and walked back to the guesthouse. Around dusk I asked

Magdoweel if I could rent his small rowboat. "Where do you want to go? Indian River again?" he asked.

"Yes," I said, "I'd like to do a little swamp research like I did in Louisiana."

"What research can you do with no equipment?" he asked. He seemed to sense the lack of complete honesty in my voice.

"I just want to do a few simple observations," I said knowing that he wasn't going to believe it.

"You saw it, didn't you?" he asked.

"Saw what?" I responded knowing then that he too must have seen the "phenomenon" I wanted to go back and check out. He gave me a "game's over" look. I said, "Okay, Magdoweel, you're right. I saw something, and I want to find out what it was."

"Is," he said.

"Do you think it was a zombie?" I asked.

"What do you think?" he asked.

"I don't believe in the walking dead, nor do I believe in the flying dead."

"But you saw."

"Yes, I saw."

"We go together," he said.

The delicate green stars, the mamaglow zone, the mangle corridor—all seemed the same as they had the night before, but Cheryl's cheeriness was with her, and Rhonda's innocence was with her, none of it with me, and I felt vulnerable. I was locked into speculative permutations, endless attempts to explain away to myself something I knew to have no explanation. I scanned my memories of Biblical studies, ghost stories, science fiction movies, horror shows, mythology, anything that could explain what I had seen. Perhaps I could forget for a few moments in the daytime, perhaps I could function, but not at night; I was becoming the shadow, the flying tormented spirit of the Diablotin Jzhombie, obsessed by its single consciousness, its lone awareness, its total feeling of final terror.

Magdoweel's rowing was becoming hypnotic. A sulphurous breath rippled the sea swells, reflecting the moon in tiny flashes like a warbling mirror ball undergoing the last stages of its unwinding and flattening into a Mercator projection. The larger moon flashes strobed with a common, rapid frequency but the smaller ones flickered with slower, more random winks. The boat was moving in thrusts through invisible, prickly Stygian electric barriers. Ancient fragrances drifted through our bodies; the darkness became complete, the silence became complete. We drifted on more slowly; we stopped. The void was complete.

On the edge of our trance appeared a winged figure. He was obscure, dark, eyeless, and evil.

"Do you know who I am?"

"Yes."

"Do you know why I am here?"

"Yes."

"Do you know yet why you are here?"

I dreamed deeply beyond the human spirit.

CHAPTER FOURTEEN

BACK TO REALITY

"Hey, Redneck! Man, ain't you a cool head!
Those things you say and do,
Oughta make Papa real proud of you!"
Atlanta Rhythm Section, Georgia, mid-seventies

I awoke back in Douglas Guest House. I was soaked. I felt shaky and tried to remember and write down what I could. I took a shower, got dressed, and went down into the street. Bob was coming back from his boat. He was going to have to fly back to St. Lucia and try to get someone else to come in and try to fix the engine. We went back to the Guest House and talked. He was hoping that we could put together his boats and my trade shuttle idea in a combination that would help everyone. The West Indians could get clean rice, fiber, shoes, and clothing (as well as more new jobs). Louisiana would have a new source of fresh, naturally grown and ripened fruit. Everyone would be paying reasonable prices, and we, of course, would get rich. The first step would have to be putting together a prospectus for the investors, the ones he already had lined up and any I could get interested. To help in that task I would need to get to St. Lucia and that would be possible if I moved to the boat, helped Gaspar guard it and helped the engineers fix it. Then, when the boat left Portsmouth so would I. It sounded like a good plan, and I was down to about a hundred dollars. That made it sound excellent.

Bob left having to pay sixty dollars for a cab to the airport. I checked out of the guesthouse, and the Aguapa crew rowed me and my stuff out to the freighter. It was not very large, about ninety feet long, with auxiliary sails. The engine that had been ruined was a single piston Diesel, very strong and reliable. I know the theory behind most engines, but I have little repair experience. Still, I could see that it was a very simple engine. I read the manual. The operating instructions were adequate and straightforward. In the "Troubleshooting" section the problem the engine was having was described as being possibly caused by running the engine too long at too slow a speed. I asked Gaspar what the engine sounded like when it was running. He described a chug-chug of about one-fourth the number of revolutions per minute that the book described as being proper. I asked him if anyone had read the book. He said that Bob had. Poor Bob, I thought. "If you want something done right, you might as well do it yourself," was an old adage that I knew he must have rolled over in his mind hundreds of times since he found out about his engine.

I got Gaspar to help me try to start the engine with a couple of the few remaining "firecrackers" left by the crew. The small explosive charge was supposed to turn the engine over sufficiently for it to compress the fuel-air mixture and then also light it off creating a self-perpetuating cycle. As Gaspar had told me, it was not going to work, book or no book.

Gaspar showed me to my bunk in the forward room of the ship, the forecastle. It was a small, deep room reached by a narrow ladder down from the deck. At my bunk there was a strong odor of spoiling fruit; the odor was leaking forward from the cargo hold. I started wheezing again. I stashed my bags and climbed back up onto the deck.

Gaspar was very upset. The cargo of fruit that filled the hold of the ship was not only spoiling but generating a lot of heat. There was the possibility of spontaneous combustion. If the fruit caught fire, the freighter would burn and sink in the harbor. Gaspar had hired the Aguapa crew to help him throw boxes of cargo overboard as he would bring them up from the hold. The boxes ruptured as they hit the water. The tide was going out. "Hands" of bananas and soggy cardboard started snaking westward out toward the horizon. I asked Gaspar how much they were going to lose. "All of it, thousands," he said pragmatically. I started pitching boxes overboard, too.

As I watched each box of bananas or mangoes burst open hitting the ocean and its contents begin to separate and create slicks and sheens shifting with the wind and currents, I had thoughts of the movements of substances at various scales. Whether at the subatomic, molecular, nano-, micro-, macro- or any level, substances affecting each other as they moved across and along interfaces, some meant to be, others interloping and intrusive requiring compensation or mitigation or remediation or just failure... I began to feel the grief that Gaspar did not show. I saw a distant frigate bird approach Dominica but move along and away as if he were annoyed that the island and its human disorders had blemished his transoceanic pathway.

Some mechanics from Roseau showed up in a hired launch. Bob had found them on his way out somehow and told them to come take a look. I could see that they had never seen a Danish Diesel engine before. They shook their heads and said, "Get a Caterpillar." They left.

The Aguapa crew had begun to play, diving overboard into the beautiful, light blue-green crystal clear water. They were joking about an endless set of unlikely subjects. I wondered how they had been able to avoid becoming zombies like some of the young men I had seen in Roseau. I was certain that the sense of humor was a most important part of the answer. Another was that they were constantly discovering new things to do or new ways to do the same old things. They never let their minds stagnate; they were aggressive with their intellects but careful not to let it become a physical aggression. I became increasingly impressed with those young men. We would work pitching cargo overboard, then rest and swim, then work some more.

After dusk Gaspar cooked a full meal which was delicious, very nearly like the "country" cooking my grandmother used to do, something like "soul food." While we were enjoying the feast, I asked the Indian River crew what would be the best cargo that could ever arrive in Portsmouth on a freighter like we were on. They all said simultaneously, "Shoes!" They explained that the rocks cut their feet but the Syrian retail cartel had priced shoes out of the range of most families. How sad, I thought, what a simple request, and I cannot make it happen, not yet. I promised them that if I ever had the chance to go back to America and set up something for Dominica, my main priority would be shoes.

The air had cleared up a little in the forecastle, but I still had to take an asthma pill to get to try to sleep. As my thoughts began to fragment I became aware, vaguely, of some dormant or silent somethings, very large and amorphous blobs within the sea. There were several of them offshore, each about two miles in diameter, maybe a mile in width and a mile in thickness, with their tops near the depth where light during the day had no longer reached down through the water. The great ovoid things were flexing with the movements of the sea, slightly shearing at their edges as current swirls would tear at them. I decided that they must have been massive microbial assemblages of some kind, generating a coherent electrical signal, their own mass spirit.

Next day we continued ditching the cargo which, because the tide had changed, began surrounding the freighter. I was debating with myself about whether I should go ashore and try to catch a transport up to the waterfalls, the boiling lake, the rain forest research station, all the things I had not yet seen, or whether I should just sit tight for a couple of days in case Gaspar had any trouble with the former crew who were apparently still on the island. I thought of how easy it would have been to get the engine fixed at home. I thought of Bob's goal of bigger freighters with refrigerated holds, twin engines, the works, the right idea. I decided to stay with the boat. At one point to cool off, I went overboard with my camera, a Nikonos, and took a picture of the beautiful benthic scene beneath us, fish, coral, and submerged vegetation.

In the wheelhouse I found and figured out the radio. I dialed in a music station, Radio Antilles out of Antigua. I had heard no news of the "outside world" in days. I began to have a craving for the news. Hour after hour passed, and there was no news broadcast. I asked Martin, and he said I would have to wait a while longer.

A few minutes before news time a rowboat came over from a dirty black motorsailer that had moored nearby. In the rowboat were two men.

One was a former crew member, Trevor, the former captain of Bob's freighter. The other was a smart-mouthed young man from Portsmouth, well known to the Aguapa crew. His name was Dick. Martin and Alec were wary of him. Dick climbed aboard and started yelling something in Patois. Then he went over and changed stations on the radio. I went over and changed it back telling him I was waiting for the news. He sneered, "You will hear news soon enough." Then he started telling Gaspar something in Patois, and Gaspar threatened to throw him to the barracudas. They started wrestling and Trevor, the former captain, jumped aboard to bail out his fellow St. Lucian. It wasn't necessary, Gaspar had Dick well in hand. Trevor and Gaspar then left Dick sitting in a pile of rotten bananas and went forward to talk. I went nearer to the radio speaker because the news was already overdue.

Dick started a new argument in Patois with Alec and Martin. It was so loud that I couldn't hear anything. Dick was claiming he had some kind of police ID. I went back and was ready to kick Dick square in the nuts and throw him to the barracudas myself when Gaspar stepped in and said something in Patois. There was another short struggle, and Dick ended up in his rowboat pulling himself back toward the motorsailer. He got out of banana range and yelled something else. Alec and Martin started after him in their rowboat. They chased him enough to let him know that his smart mouth had gotten him into another bind.

Things calmed down and I thought about Gaspar's leadership qualities. He was in his mid-twenties. Everyone in Portsmouth seemed to respect him partly because of his looks (the ladies of town all seemed to be more than just casually interested in him), partly for his education (which he wouldn't have been able to receive on Dominica), partly for his obvious financial success. He dressed in the latest styles available on the islands. He wore good boots and colorful "threads." The blacks of Portsmouth saw in Gaspar what they had wanted to show the English all those years when it could not have happened. When Gaspar talked, the St. Lucian sound overrode his Patois, and the people listened.

Gaspar was what the Republicans call "executive material." He was a convinced capitalist and he, like his mentor, Bob, taught and preached ambition constantly. But Gaspar was a West Indian and people listened and heard from him what they would not hear from Bob. Bob must have seen that years ago. I could see why Gaspar wasn't worried about getting fired.

Gaspar and Trevor came back to the wheelhouse and explained that for some reason, the bank had taken the crew's checks and then wouldn't cash them. Gaspar and Trevor would have to go into town in the morning and try to reach Bob if they could get an overseas call through from Portsmouth. Otherwise, they would have to go to Roseau to the overseas telephone and telegraph office. In the meantime Gaspar had agreed to subsidize the stranded crewmen until we could figure out was "developing" and what to do about it. I asked, "What IS developing?" The St. Lucians explained that a general strike had been declared on their home island and that Trevor had had to spend the night with the Portsmouth Police.

I said that I had had similar confusion with the bank and the police. We all seemed to be considered some kind of suspects even before we met each other. Now that their country was in a state of turmoil and the police had probably heard where I was, with other suspicious characters, we all were probably doubly suspect.

What was it all about? None of us had done anything to anyone on Dominica, that is, not until we had to threaten to throw the Junior Deputy Dick to the barracudas... We began to go back over our experiences trying to figure it out. I really craved for some news.

"This is Radio Antilles News. In New Orleans today the FBI arrested ten American mercenaries for attempting to invade the small island nation of Dominica in the Caribbean. The terrorists, reportedly from Texas, Louisiana, and Quebec were well armed, completely equipped, and are believed to have accomplices already on the island of Dominica. They were apparently part of a conspiracy to overthrow the duly elected government of that country. The FBI had notified the government of Prime Minister Eugenia Charles some time in advance of the arrests. Prime Minister Charles has made no statement yet concerning the attempted invasion... On St. Lucia there is widespread unrest in the wake of today's sudden general strike... On the Bahamas a wildcat strike threatens to shut down tourism... In El Salvador..."

The news that I had been craving hit me like a cosmic slap across the face. I had had green lights all the way to Dominica and now this? I was stunned and angry.

What kind of idiots would have gotten themselves busted in my home state trying to invade Dominica? Not one person got arrested along our entire coastline during the launching of the Bay of Pigs invasion. I kept thinking. Bay of Pigs invasion nothing—that had ended up looking like an old-fashioned setup. "That's what this has to be, same script, refined, detuned, simplified, probably the same producers," I thought, not angry at the patsies but very resentful of the silent, heartless, self-grading "intelligence" characters that played with innocent lives.

Gaspar said, "Did they say invasion of Dominica?" I turned the radio down and then off.

"Yes, stopped by the FBI," I said.

Trevor said, "Where?"

I said, "Louisiana."

The Aguapa crew whispered to each other, and then Martin said, "You are from Louisiana, aren't you?"

I nodded, "Yes."

Alec said, "From the same town the invaders are from?"

"I don't know. They were caught in New Orleans. That's where I caught the plane, but that's not where I'm from. My home is Calcasieu Parish, two hundred miles west, by Texas."

"Texas, lots of gunmen in Texas," said Martin, and he got that zombie-fear look again.

"I'm not part of the invasion, but at least we know why I've been under surveillance. And that could also explain some of your problems, Trevor and Gaspar." It all began to fit together. We all thought it through silently. The government on St. Lucia was probably warning the other islands of impending revolution. The FBI was warning Dominica to watch out for anyone from Louisiana. We were all on the same freighter, throwing the top layer of cargo overboard, asking for topographic maps, making day and night runs up the only navigable river on Dominica. We were in the best strategic position on the island for most purposes. We could easily cut the last unwashed-out road between the capital and the airport if troops were flown in to protect the Eugenia Charles government. The Dominican Defense Force, their Army, had supposedly recently traded away their weapons to the "Dreads" in return for hashish, and we had been seen talking to Rastas and Rasta sympathizers. Customs had probably seen me smile and nod at the white guys working on the old Seagreen DC-3 when I landed at the airport. I finally knew what was going on. I was imagining what else might be going on. I was getting paranoid. We all were.

Gaspar decided that it was time to break out one of the last unspoiled crates of magnificent chule mangoes from the cargo hold. We started stuffing ourselves juicily. The Aguapa crew got their smiles back and said something in Patois to Gaspar and Trevor, something like, "You fellas better *laissez le bon temps rouler* while you still can." Trevor threw mango seeds at them, and they jumped overboard laughing. Martin got the rowboat and said: "Let's go tell Magdoweel!"

"Just Magdoweel!" I yelled after them. "Don't tell anybody but Magdoweel!"

Chapter Fifteen

Back to Roseau/Back to Hell

"I'm just walkin' in this rain
Thinking about my life and thangs.
The rain hides my tears and pain.
I'm just walkin' in this rain."
Lowell Fulsom, Shreveport, fifties

Gaspar, Trevor, and I had a conference. Perhaps it would be possible to get a call through tonight to Bob from Portsmouth. The only phone, other than the bank and the police station, was at the disco. They would be open soon. Gaspar could guard the boat while Trevor and I would take the dinghy into the rear of the disco. Gaspar asked if I had a gun to leave with him, and I had to explain again about the Rod and Gun Club patch. Trevor and I left.

We got the call through. A cheerful Bob said, "Mike, I'm surprised you haven't been arrested...at least." I didn't think it was too funny. He asked if I knew any of the "invaders." I said that I hadn't heard the names yet but that I didn't think that any of my acquaintances were the type to get busted in New Orleans on an invasion charge. Then I told him his crew's money had been suspended by the bank in Portsmouth. That pissed him off. He said he'd try to straighten it out in the morning, general strike permitting. Trevor relayed some messages for Gaspar and got some extra reassurances about the money situation. I began to get the feeling that those same men who were about ready to have gone to any extremes against each other over a financial difference less than forty-eight hours earlier, had now rejoined forces when unfairly confronted simultaneously by the same adversary. I was reassured that I must be with the right group and that, if we could just have some time to figure things out, we would figure them out and then we would help each other make the right moves, the most efficient, least disruptive, most just moves to insure our own survival.

Bob told Trevor that Gaspar and I should get into Roseau next morning early and take care of our business there. (Mine, of course, would be getting my stuff out of the Cherry Lodge without getting picked up. Gaspar's was their business; he would know what to do.) Trevor and I rowed back through the darkness to the freighter. Gaspar had been trying again to start the engine. It was hopeless. We were not going to get out that way.

Trevor slept in the wheelhouse; I slept on deck, and Gaspar slept in the forecastle. I got rained on; it felt pretty good, then it cleared up. I again saw the billions of stars. I pulled a tarp over me and fell back asleep.

Next morning Trevor started reworking the sail rigging. I asked how fast she would go under just sail. "Not fast enough if anyone chases us. Not fast enough if we get near storm."

"Hmm," I thought, "maybe while I'm in Roseau, I should ask Andy how he'd like to come up to Portsmouth and teach us some sailing tricks. We could drop him off back ashore near Roseau as we pass to the south." Gaspar was ready. We rowed in to Portsmouth. Martin met us on the beach and said something about it not being safe to try to get a cab. We would have to hitch. I began getting a very bad feeling beyond the realization that I might be arrested or worse.

We caught a couple of short dangerous rides; then, thankfully, we got a ride with the Dean of the medical school and his excellent driver. I had known about the med school from my readings and had intended to visit and photograph it, eventually. "Where are you from?" asked the Dean after the preliminary introductions.

"Louisiana," I said; then for the first time in my life I felt like unsaying it, wondering if he'd heard about the invasion. He must not have.

I changed the subject. "I flunked out of LSU Med School in 1966."

"Really?" said the Dean, a little surprised.

"Yeah, biochemistry, I didn't feel like memorizing charts."

"Well, we have a nice biochemistry course here; maybe you'd like to take it if you are going to be around for a while."

"No, thanks," I said. "Twice is enough; besides, I won't be around here very long." I looked at Gaspar, and he knew that that was an optimistic statement.

We reached the Castaways Campus at Mero, thanked the Dean for the ride, and complimented the chauffeur. Then we started hitchhiking again. We had to walk a few miles before we got another ride, a short one to an intersection where we then caught a small open transport, something like a minibus, right away. Gaspar called it a jitney. I thought about the odd preservation of old English words in places like the Caribbean and Willow Springs, Louisiana. I wondered why such words were lost in the more "advanced" places.

About a mile from Goodwill we came upon a fresh cave-in. The road was only one lane wide, the ocean was down to the right. Trucks and cars from each direction were trying to squeeze past each other. We got all blocked up. No one could maneuver backward or forward. The traffic began stacking up behind us and ahead of us coming from town. Everyone started blowing their horns and screaming at each other and cursing. Gaspar became thoroughly exasperated. "Nothing like this could happen on St. Lucia! Nothing! Fifty years backward! Primitive! This place is fifty years backward!"

One old lady in the transport was getting frightened. She said to her friend, "No human compassion, no more human compassion."

Even though, surrounded as I was, in such close quarters, by people of different backgrounds, and therefore again sensing that feeling of being a member of "the minority," I got a deep feeling of resignation, something I found to be unfamiliar, a novelty, an internal paradox. I said, "Gaspar, this is too fluky, this is a cosmic delay; it's out of our hands, it's a cosmic cave-in. We may never know the reason, but there is a reason." I would know the reason for the delay within an hour.

The traffic jam was solved when someone in Roseau decided to get to the cause of the stoppage and to do so had to make their line back up. My bad feeling was worse, my resignation evaporated.

I was irritable and anxious. I decided I would have to risk leaving my alleyway route to the Cherry Lodge when I got out of the transport and instead go on to the overseas telephone office and call home. I was having one of those rare "intuitions" that I had learned not to ignore. I knew without knowing why that I had to call home. Gaspar didn't like that idea but said he might as well go along and try to get another call through to Bob.

I got my call through. My brother-in-law Tom answered. He said that it was strange that I should call now. Only five minutes before he had found out that one of my sons had been seriously injured. "How serious is it?" I asked. Tom didn't have the details yet; it was an eye injury. "How did it happen?" I asked.

"Battery acid," he said, "that's all we've heard so far." I told Tom to tell my injured child that I was coming right home as soon as I could but that there was a problem; I wasn't sure how long it would take.

Tom hesitated, then said, "Then, you've heard the news?"

"Just a while ago."

"Did you know any of ..."

"The names weren't announced here, but I do know that they've messed me up whoever they are."

"Can we help?"

"Call the American Embassy if you don't hear from me within a couple of days."

"Okay, good luck."

"Thanks, Tom, see you all soon, I hope. Tell everyone I love them. Goodbye."

Gaspar got through to Bob. After discussing their situation, Gaspar gave me the phone so I could talk with Bob. I told him of my son's injury and that I was going to have to try the airport route out once Gaspar and I made it back to Portsmouth. Bob said that he understood and hoped we would be in touch later. So did I. He and Gaspar talked some final business, and we quickly left the telephone office.

It was raining again. I was beginning to feel a sadness I had hoped I never would have to feel. My son was injured. I was helpless. I might not even be able to get back to him. What kind of fool had I become? I thought back to those nights in San Francisco where my former wife and I talked about the sadness that could come along with the joy of having new loved ones sparkling up our lives. We decided that the joys must be paramount, that the Creator would help. We had decided to have children.

Gaspar and I split up just before we reached the Cherry Lodge. He said that he wasn't going to ride any more "crowded damn Japanese jitney back to Portsmouth." He was going to find a "real car." I hoped that he would also find a real driver. I went on to the Cherry Lodge. I found the lady who had sent my laundry out to be hand washed, probably at one of the rivers. She said that the laundry was back, and I paid her $5 more, US. The Diesel smell was gone. Some poor old lady had really earned her $15. I thought that maybe someday I would get her a real laundromat.

I tugged all my stuff out of the attic and downstairs. I looked at the magnificent little bamboo boat. If it hadn't been for that boat, I probably wouldn't have risked going back to Roseau. I wouldn't have known about my son's accident back home. I stashed everything near the side door. I sneaked over to the music shop and picked up my custom tape. It was still raining. Gaspar came along and said we would have to carry all my stuff to the car; the driver didn't want to drive up at the Cherry Lodge. "Why?" I asked.

Gaspar said, "Let's just hurry, come on." We sneaked back into the Cherry Lodge and got my things and sneaked over a few blocks to the car.

The "real car" was an overpowered beast of a Pontiac, maybe ten years old. Its muffler, like most on Dominica, was gone, and it sounded like a one vehicle drag race. The "driver" said nothing. He was extremely nervous. Gaspar sat up front, and I rode in the back. I couldn't find a seat belt, car too old I guessed. We started another one of those idiotic nightmare rides, too fast, too near the limits of the machine, beyond the limits of everything but the driver's luck.

We got to Portsmouth too fast, but we got there. Gaspar pulled out a fresh wad of green money and peeled off some for the driver as we unloaded by the dinghy. We saw Martin and asked him to go back into town to get the rest of the Aguapa crew. I wanted them to come out to the boat so that I could split up my camping gear among them. Gaspar and I rowed back to the freighter. I gave almost all the rest of my stuff to Gaspar so that I could travel light. All I kept was the little boat, the Niconos camera, the tape recorder and cassettes, and my daypack. I was going to have enough trouble getting the little bamboo boat back intact as it was, without all the other baggage.

It was dark again. The Aguapa crew rowed up, collected their new equipment, then gave me a ride back to shore. They pointed out the proper hitchhiking spot. Several vehicles passed but did not stop. An hour passed. I began to feel stranded again. I thought of the night that Claire got captured on the beach in Cameron Parish leaving me stranded on a chenier ridge. I had been worried sick about her like I was now worried about my wounded son. I prayed for him as I had prayed for her, hoping that he could somehow come through as well as she had (knowing that I may have already prayed for all the miracles I am entitled to). I remembered the same helpless feeling, and I remembered the arrival of the three Army men on their motorcycles just before midnight, just before it would have been too late, a twentieth century cavalry. I remember powering out of "the wrong place at the right time" and the confrontation we had with the "deputies" who told our leader, "We don't allow no nigger bikers down this road at night," and I remember the second mad dash to the federal installation on the Hackberry salt dome. Then I remembered the helicopter ride when we almost caught the petroleum reserve saboteurs red-handed. Why was I always in the big middle of everything I didn't know about in advance?

There would be no U.S. Cavalry dashing in on porcine machines tonight. I was "on vacation." I was on my own. Not even Claire knew where I was. My mind was oscillating from old to new realities, from new to old fears, from old to new and through the timeless ones…

CHAPTER SIXTEEN

―――

RASTAS ARE NICE PEOPLE

"I've got a lot of Rasta friends
around my place in Jamaica,
they watch it, they take care of me,
Rasta's are nice people."
Keith Richard of the Rolling Stones, England, 1981

I could tell that I wasn't going to get a ride. I knew that I had to be at the airport when it opened in the morning. I would have to get myself on the top of the standby list for the first flight out and hope that I didn't get arrested. I felt certain that the more hours spent on Dominica, the more likely it was that I would get picked up for questioning in the invasion. I would not be able to climb all the way up and over the mountains and still be able to get to the airport in time. I noticed that loaded banana trucks were coming downhill, going around the curve, then coming back empty and passing me up. I walked the road until I found their unloading terminal.

Several Rastafarians were finishing their day's work unloading the banana trucks. I asked about a ride to the Melville Hall Airport. The Rastas all seemed to notice the little bamboo boat I was carefully cradling in my left arm, but they did not mention it. I was directed to one of the workers who lived in that direction. He and several other laborers were going to ride in the back of one of the trucks all the way up to their homes. He also noticed the little boat then said that I could ride with them in the back of the unloaded truck on the way to the summit. That would be as far as I could ride and from there, I could take my chances on getting another ride. He wanted to hear the little tape recorder. I began playing one of the tapes. The driver was ready to leave. We climbed aboard and hauled ass uphill.

The banana truck was "a real truck," a beautifully engineered Ford cab-over, six-wheeled, plenty powerful and tough. I knew that we weren't likely to run into anything bigger except maybe the island itself. We roared around the hairpins on the deserted mountain road. We dived into little valleys, slid through the bottom of the curves, and then gunned its nose up again. I was back in 1967, back on the road from Fresno to Yosemite, wide open and not worried about it. I thought, "This man drives like I do. This man drives the vehicle, not his luck!"

I had ridden into Roseau in the hands of the devil, and I was riding out of Portsmouth in the hands of the Lord, or was it vice-versa? It didn't matter, I felt safe, and I was no longer stranded.

My companions were really grooving, too; we were all loving the twirling stars, the spinning mountain walls, the positive and negative g's of the ride, and the reggae tape. We climbed into the night mist zone. Suddenly the driver locked up the brakes. We slid a long way on the wet pavement. We stopped and then began backing up. I looked over at the workers, and they gestured puzzlement too. I shut off the tape. We stopped backing up. The driver got out and walked to the bushes beside the road. He picked up the small body of a manicou, a Dominican 'possum, and threw it into the back of the truck with us and then went back to driving. "Manicou, good with provisions," one of my fellow travelers said. Just like fresh 'possum back home, I thought, good with turnips (if you drain off all the poison fat).

We got to the summit, and the Rastas thanked me for letting them listen to the tape. I gave them the cassette recorder and thanked them all for the ride. I told them that I hoped they enjoyed the possum. "Manicou," they said. "Manicou," I waved as they roared away toward their village.

I had made it to the Angel's Saddle. It was nearly midnight. I had eight hours and only a few miles to cover if I used a walking trail shortcut instead of the highway. Since I had seen no other vehicles on the road that night I started hiking the short cut. It was too dark to use the topo map, so I was glad that I had already memorized the major trails. I tried to walk as quietly as I could. "No need to attract the Dreads on top of all the rest of this fiasco," I told myself. I paced myself. I was still out of shape, but I knew that I could make the downhill miles in eight hours.

Major trails in Dominica are not as major as they are in Glacier Park. However, my lungs were holding up fine, my feet had toughened up, my skydiving-shattered ankle was still holding together thanks to Dr. Philips of the Delta Chapter of the Sierra Club and his careful skills. My spirit was holding up. As long as I was within a fair shot at my target, I was confident that I would hit it. I was going to make it.

Why did I have to tell myself that? I wondered. Why do I always end up chastising myself or with self-doubts that I should have never considered in the first place? The walking became more difficult. After a couple of hours my calves began to feel heavy, and I thought of cutting away from the short-cut back to the road. My ankle was beginning to swell, and my lungs began to overheat even in the cool night mist. I could hear no vehicles. Nothing was running at this time of night probably anywhere on Dominica. I had to remind myself that there shouldn't be. "Let the animals have a few hours of peace." I began to fantasize as I hiked onward: "What if the zombies are really in Fond Zombie, the Zombie Bottoms? It should be just behind me over that ridge... Well, I just walked past it, and no zombies got me... What if I had remembered its name—the Diablotin Jzhombie—what was it?... At last I'm getting to hike... Still need to go camping... It would be so nice to have Elena with me again... I wonder if she's still writing for Chavez out in California?... I wonder if there are really 'Dreads' out here in the bush? ... Waiting to grab me... kidnap me... I wonder if there are any Amazons in the bush..." I kept walking, but I could no longer find a workable pace. Still, I knew that I had to make those miles.

On the starlit trail ahead stood two very large Negroes. One had a shaved head and looked like Mr. Clean. The other had "Dreadlocks" and looked like Medusa. "Hidy," I said, and walked on up to them.

"What are you doing here?" asked Mr. Clean.

"I'm trying to get home to see my children. I found out today that one got hurt."

Both men were staring at the bamboo boat.

"Where are your children?"

"Louisiana."

They looked at each other. Mr. Clean said, "Follow me." Medusa fell in behind me.

"Well, these are awfully nice kidnappers," I thought. We headed up Morne Diablotins and went far into the elfin woodland of the cloud zone. The trail was nearly imperceptible. Mr. Clean walked like it was daytime. I could hardly hear Medusa.

We came upon a beautifully camouflaged encampment with its own portable hydroelectric stereo system with eight sets of earphones. It was more than just a stereo system. The other components were a little more functional, a clandestine communications node. Somehow I knew that I was still in the right hands. I was taken to an older "Dread."

He saw the magnificent little boat and smiled at his people. Then he asked me to tell him how I came to be in the rainforest in the middle of the night. I explained the situation as completely as he wanted me to. He was quite compassionate and set up a way for me to get to the airport more easily. It would be in a small car with an inconspicuous member of their clan, one who served as a secret interface between the fugitives and Dominica's "real world." I thanked the Dread leader and invited him and all his people to Louisiana.

While I was in the dimly lit Dread compound I noticed that some of the Dreads had really large, muscular feet, perhaps hyperdeveloped from their barefoot mountain trekking. If I ever did get a shipment of shoes for the island, it would have to include a lot of super shoes for the super people. Then I thought, maybe they would not want to fix what is not broken...I did not ask.

On the way to the airport my short haired Rasta guide explained that the "Dreads" were on the run in their own country because they smoked ganja, a kind of marijuana for which the government had a paranoid fear.

I told him that I could relate to that in a way. The police had beat them, shaved their heads publicly, shocked their genitals—it all sounded familiar. Self-defeating overreaction, "When will they ever learn?" I told him that the voters were fighting that kind of injustice in the United States. He smiled a tragic smile and said that he wished that it could work like that on Dominica. I asked him why it couldn't. "We are the minority. Roseau has the votes."

It hit me! Roseau had the votes! That's why all those people were being kept there, undispersed, dependent upon a very few puppeteers, modern political slave masters who controlled things by electing and rejecting governments at will, a nominal "democracy," made vulgar and obscene by greed... I said, "I've been to Roseau, I know why the French burned it down." He said, "We know, too."

We continued on silently for a while. I asked him, "How do you feel about the crop dusting plane I saw parked at the airport?"

"We don't plan to stimulate any Agent Orange drops if we can help it," he said, telling me in that quick way that my environmental concern over DDT contamination of the ecosystem, although valid, was subordinate to a real threat of massive defoliation for which the big shots' puppet propaganda team might blame the Dreads. I saw that it could be another Viet Nam, with the defoliated magnificent forests going up for bids as "salvage."

The dreaded Rastafarian told me that the police had rounded up some Americans, even some of the nurses from the hospital and the medical school. He said that he had heard that one of the women was, for some reason, being held in a dungeon. I wondered if she were the one I had seen assisting back at the Princess Margaret Hospital. Poor girl, she was only trying to help.

The Highlands were in thoughtful hands. I wished I could introduce these men to Emerson Watty. I thought that a truly thoughtful dialogue would be inevitable should the wise elders and wise youth ever meet outside the presence of the unwise. I thought of that in terms of the "spiritual realm" as well as in our "real world."

We neared the perimeter of the airport and stopped in a coconut plantation. I gave the secret Dread a picture of Claire with some of her hearing testimony sayings written on the back: "WE THE PEOPLE LOVE THE EARTH' and "We are trading the old way of life for new ways of death."

He read them, looked at her again and said, "She is a beautiful person."

I said, "Yes, she is, and so are y'all. Rastas are nice people."

He smiled and as he waved me on toward the airfield, I thought I could sense some kind of pride the man was feeling as he watched a little Rasta boat get ready to sail to a world that needed its blessings. It was one of those "delusional" moments I'd been trained by our so-called civilization to ignore, something irrational, unscientific, unreal.

I slipped through a hole in the unrepaired Hurricane David-damaged hurricane fence. The sun was coming up over the ocean end of the runway. I'm going to make it; I reassured myself, "Rastas are nice people."

Chapter Seventeen

Escape from Escape

"Exodus...movement of Jah people..." Bob Marley,
A Caribbean Island, 1977

"How could all this be happening?" I kept asking myself. I really did have cosmic green lights all the way to Dominica, then, blam, no amber lights, just red, very red. After five years of trying to get away from high tension, controversial, tightrope activism, for a vacation I was given an eight day nightmare. No, actually I really did get that one day of rest, that beautiful river tour, the incredible zombie hunt, the new friends.

I walked the center of the runway toward the terminal thinking that I must be crazy to think I could actually just pass as an airline customer. Still, I had to try it that way. The only other way seemed to be stealing the biocide plane. I have always been disgusted by thieves. Yet Jesus forgave them or maybe just one of them and left the rest for us to forgive. I walked on past the toxic plane.

The sun was climbing up into the clouds which blew into existence as the tropical trade winds still collided with the island and tried to climb over it leaving the heavy water vapor to fall into the rivers. There are some things that should never change. I looked out that eastern slot between the cloud cover and the clear horizon. I stopped and stared toward that clear window to freedom wondering if I would make it off the end of the runway. I turned and looked toward the west to the green jungle, the home of the Zombies and up toward the mountains, still shrouded in grey fog and rain, home of the Rastas. I looked to the south, to the drenched Sisserou parrot on the soaked flag left overnight to guard the planes of the twentieth century. It was the only Sisserou I had seen. Would that parrot become extinct like another state bird, Louisiana's pelican? Would politics continue to embarrass itself and destroy us?

No, the spirit of the Flower Children is alive on Dominica. The soul of the Acadian is alive on Dominica. Love is alive on Dominica. The Highlands are in good hands I kept telling myself. The Indian River is in good hands. Tropicrafts is in good hands. Andy's boats are in good hands. The theatre group is in good hands. There were many people with good hands on Dominica, people with good, strong souls defiantly safe from the hungry evil that watched and stalked them jealously.

I walked around to the locked front door of the Melville Hall terminal. I was there first. I took off my daypack and carefully rested the little bamboo boat on top of it. I stretched out on the step and rested.

People began to arrive, Americans looking shaken from the twenty-five mile taxi fright, and Dominicans looking festive, carrying bundles of fresh cut flowers celebrating their own escapes, I supposed. Workers arrived. Police and customs officials arrived. The airport began to wake up.

The door opened, and I went to the LIAT counter. I explained that I had an open ticket but no reservation since I was leaving to go back home early because of a family emergency. I explained that I would like to get the first flight. I was put down as Standby #1. A pretty young lady with a nearly Cajun accent was put down as Standby #2. She was wearing a light yellow, lacy summer dress that amplified her queenly aura perfectly. She looked at me and the little boat and I thought I saw her grin as she looked away. A sweaty, string-tied, open-collared businessman in cowboy boots was put down as Standby #3. I saw the cosmic game being played again: Louisiana, Quebec, Texas, Standbys 1,2,3, the very set of invaders the Great Communicator had warned the Dominicans to watch for. I told the cosmic chess players that I hoped that they were getting a charge out of this, didn't it ever get old? Apparently the three of us all had similarly accelerated departure requirements or perhaps all international airports are cold places, filled with people in crises. Soon the many locally originating standbys were given boarding passes: Numbers 1, 2, and 3 were not. Uniformed men with machine guns arrived and began staring at us.

I looked at the sweaty American who was trying to stealthily wring his hands and gnash his teeth. I looked at the beautiful Bardot who had begun pouting. I hoped we could share a cell... I straightened out my thinking, but I felt better as I told myself, "Well, you are still alive if you can still see her through that incredible lace outfit she is wearing." I decided that she and I were going to make it out of there together. This was going to be nice; it was rather obvious. She was outstanding. I heard her tell the ticket agent that her name was Lili. She was fine!

Lili looked like the Mademoiselle from Armentières, but she had become angry, true Cajun mad. She had confronted the LIAT agents about not getting a boarding pass. I went up to the ticket counter and verified that I, too, had been bumped out of my standby position and would not be allowed to leave on the morning plane, family emergency at home or not. "Maybe you be released for the afternoon plane."

I tried not to glare. I said, "It means nothing to you people that I have a family emergency, does it?" I did glare; the ticket agents froze and played zombie as I assured them with my eyes that they'd played the wrong card, very wrong. I realized that in that moment I had become the very kind of American that I had scorned, the spoiled brat who could not get his way and so he attacked the innocent, and made enemies for himself and his country. Too late, I thought—for every reaction there is an equal and opposite reaction.

I turned and introduced myself to Lili. I asked her, "You aren't Cajun, are you?"

"No, I'm from Quebec." I was right, the cosmic game was under way. The sweaty American quietly checked his standby status and found that he was bumped, too. He got very shifty-eyed. We said nothing to each other and tried to avoid more than just the one eye-link it took to agree to join forces if we were pressed into that kind of thing. We had become and realized that we were three fellow travelers in trouble, the same trouble, and at least one of us knew that he didn't deserve it, maybe every one.

"Well, here comes a nice Seagreen DC-3, let me see what those old boys are up to!" I strode over toward the observation fence getting my camera out and looking very touristy. The DC-3 landed, the men got out and went into the restroom while cargo arrangements were being made, then started for coffee as I was practicing my opening lines: "Good morning, I saw your plane in Antigua; it's beautiful. Is it the only one? Can you fly Lili, Tex, and me off this hell of a place, fast?" While they were getting their coffee, I mentioned to Lili that we'd better be finding another way out and be ready to move fast. She nodded and went to the little Air Guadeloupe counter and started whispering in French.

In addition to considering the chance for an escape on the Seagreen company DC-3, I kept looking across the field at the old Grumman Ag-Cat with its big radial engine. I knew that the DDT spray plane, the one that the Rasta's had worried about as being used against them in a Viet Nam kind of wartime defoliation, might be my best bet. At least if I did manage to get across the runway without getting machine gunned to death, if I did manage to get the radial engine fired up, if I did manage to get it into the air but ended up ruining the plane in another one of my habitually-bad landings, the Rastas would not have to worry about contamination and defoliation for a while.

I drifted back to wondering why, if we were being bumped off the flight so we could be arrested for complicity in an invasion, why we were not already arrested. Then I heard some distant sirens. Up the road came a bunch of police Land Rovers loaded with a big bunch of police with a big bunch of bigger machine guns. The DC-3 pilots set down their unfinished coffee and went out and cranked up the old plane before I could ask for a ride. One of them gave me a long look as he delayed shutting the oversized cargo door. He seemed to be transmitting me some ESP: "Man, if you are going to make a break for it you've gotta do it now, before I shut this door! C'mon! Now! Do it!" I kept hesitating. He looked back into the plane and toward the pilot and yelled something as he pulled the door shut. The plane began rapidly taxiing away. I snapped their picture as I realized I might have missed my last chance.

Lili came up and said, "We can get tickets on Air Guadeloupe, have you the money?"

I said, "Yes, maybe just enough; that'll leave me stranded on Guadeloupe or Antigua, but I'm sure that will be more pleasant than being stranded in a Dominican dungeon."

"Yes," she said, unconvincingly: "I might get stranded there, too." She smiled as if waiting for me to submit a proposal or proposition of some kind. I was still thinking about the missed escape on the company DC-3. "Yes, well, let's buy our tickets," she said as the Land Rovers arrived.

The sweaty American followed us and also bought a ticket to ride; now all we had to do was to get past the Customs Disembarkation Man, I hoped. I thought to myself that a caravan of Land Rovers full of automatic weapons was another overreaction; certainly Lili and Tex and I couldn't look that formidable. The Customs crew had pulled away from the gate to see the arrival of the Land Rovers. They left a green kid to make sure no one left on Air Guadeloupe without getting stamped in the passport. I figured that we weren't going to have enough time to clear out and get on the Air Guadeloupe plane, which was just arriving, and then have time to get off the ground before the police got to us. "Quite a cosmic game you have going today, boys," I said to the Invisible Ones who play with our lives.

I suppressed the heretic in me and watched Lili pressing the young customs agent to hurry up; the plane had taxied up to the terminal, was waiting, and was late already, she badgered. I snapped some quick shots of the police and the guns and of all people: "Ms. Eugenia Charles, Prime Minister of Dominica."

So, the Land Rovers had something else to handle first, before us! Ms. Charles was having her moment of glory, and it was being videotaped. It would indeed make a sweet propaganda film, I thought. The dynamic woman leader leaving Dominica under heavy guard to seek outside assistance, direly needed protection from the invading hordes of robed fanatics from Louisiana! Sheesh. Nevertheless, it was an equal and opposite reaction.

Lili still hadn't cleared Customs. She was beginning to sizzle. The sweaty "Texecutive" was curling his toenails inside his Tony Lama lizard-skins, waiting to see if the agent would summon the police to grab Lili. I walked up and got in line behind her, looking impatient which I figured was better than looking panicked. Lili was holding her passport open with her thumb at just the right page tempting the young man with how easy it would be for him to place the stamp. Lili looked up to where the Aurora Borealis would have been if this were a cool night in Quebec and said something that started off like a slow, peaceful lullaby in exquisite French, and as she slowly turned her eyes down toward the young Customs agent, she began to change the tone of her voice toward that of monarchical domination as she also began to tense all her muscles looking like she was about to have the opposite of an orgasm as her temper absolutely flew raging into the poor fellow's ...mind... and he stamped her passport just in time to avoid a nasty, nasty scene. Lili plateaued in a silent Cajun burn, snatched the passport back, and swirled to the plane.

I held my passport out to the agent with my thumb holding it open at just the right page, and the rattled kid stamped it. The sweaty American had learned the same trick I'd learned from Lili, stuck his Texas passport down with his thumb holding it open at just the right page to make it easier for the customs agent to stamp than to think about it.

We were all stamped and climbing into the little twin-engined Cessna plane. I thought: "They'd better finish that propaganda flick fast; we are going to be long gone while Ms. Charles is still posing."

The pilot said to the ground crewman, "Still no sign of the other four?" The crewman shrugged. Lili said something urgent in French which probably meant "Get this——-ing plane off the ground fast, *s'il vous plaît!*" and the Texan and I nodded and gestured even though we were just guessing at the translation. The pilot hesitated momentarily as if he really hated to leave anyone on Dominica. The crewman said, "No other passengers, others no show, go."

Not-so-smiling Jacques gave in, got in, locked the door, and slowly lit the engines. Lili urged him in English this time, "My father's pilot can take an Otter off a lake half as long as this runway."

The pilot taxied, not to the end of the runway, just to the center, revved up, and said, "This isn't an Otter or a lake, and I'm not your father's pilot.

What's going on with you people, anyway?" and by then we were lifting off the ground and climbing like her daddy's pilot probably never dared.

I said, "Thanks to the Creator, my guardian angels, Air Guadeloupe, and Lili Grand Bois for getting me out of that beautiful but messed up place!"

Lili laughed and translated in French to the pilot who just shook his head saying, "Ah, Dominica, Dominica."

I reflected upon the inverted tensions of my landing and takeoff from Dominica. I had been just as determined to get off its ground than I had been to get onto its ground. Down, then up, in both directions—as I reflected I saw a reality, not just the airplanes, not just the people, but certainly the guardian angels...I will always thank them.

The sweaty American who hadn't said a word never did. His head was resting against the plane's window, and either sweat or tears were running down the Plexiglass. This time the rain was inside the plane.

Twenty minutes later we flew into the twenty-first century, Point-A-Pitre, a place so far advanced in civilization compared with Dominica that I could actually close my eyes and breathe again; I made it to Guadeloupe. It was good to know that I would soon be home with my sons.

Lili and I spent several hours together (all I could buy her was a cup of coffee). Then we flew our separate ways. I put Dominica out of my mind. From Hell to Heaven in twenty minutes! The joy was paramount! And the little bamboo boat was still in one piece.

CHAPTER EIGHTEEN

BREAK OVER

"Whiffo ya jump out dat yearohplane, man, whiffo?"
Little Black Boy, Lafourche Parish, 1966.

During my skydiving days, another disastrous time in my life, the "whiffos" would come up and bug me while I was trying to remember how Henri told me to pack the "chute." "There are only two ways, my way and the fatal way," he used to say. Henri was a benevolent dictator, a truly benevolent dictator. He knew his own weaknesses, and he knew those of his students. He knew mine, and he knew that I really wanted to jump out of an airplane with at least one functional parachute. He knew that I accepted his dictatorship because I had asked him to be that way when he knew he had to be; after all, he was the jumpmaster, I was the novice. He was structurally and intellectually intact after thousands of jumps and that one thing bought my complete loyalty, complete and with no reservations as long as we were talking skydiving.

I seldom subjugate myself to any other human being. I am disgusted by symbols of human sacrifice of their own free wills, symbols such as forty-hour workweeks, bureaus, contracts, confirmation ceremonies, anything that involves compromise when the truth is known. There should never be any compromise near the truth. Conversely, when I was skydiving, I did not know the truth, not the full and complete truth. What I did know was that there were some people who knew a lot more than I did and if I planned to hit the dirt softly and safely, I should not negotiate with such people; I had learned the hard way that I should simply hear what they had to say and if it sounded like the real reason they were alive, I would accept what they said and do it their way. Henri told me his way, he told me the truth, and I learned how to stay alive and healthy even after falling through most of the atmosphere. Only when I disobeyed did I lose the protection of wisdom. Dominica needs a Henri, someone who knows what to do, someone who can provide a matrix for orderly thought and planning, someone who cares about Life.

My original plane ticket had the required "return" to United States territory, San Juan, Puerto Rico. My brother-in-law, Tom, and my sister, Lila, bought me a ticket the rest of the way back to New Orleans. Also leaving Guadeloupe aboard the plane to Antigua, were some Seventh Day Adventist missionaries evacuating from Dominica, one of whom was muttering, "Ah, Dominica, Dominica, you never change."

During my layover in Antigua I went back to the American consulate where I had checked in previously. I wanted to talk with the same agent who had wished me luck but had let me walk right into the entire mess on Dominica. I was certain that he had known about the "invasion" even as he had been wishing me luck and letting me go forward. At first the person at the counter said I would have to make an appointment. I told her that I was going to expose the rumors of revolutions on the other islands, the whole mess for what it was, a fantasy concocted by some CIA *coullion* hash-freaks with nothing better to do but play international games with the office of the President of the United States. The woman blanched and called the man. He came out to ask me into his office. Once back in his office he said, "Spill your guts." I was so angry that a different thought crossed my mind. I restrained myself but accused him of the foreknowlege that I knew he could not deny.

He admitted that he had known I had been walking into a mess but said that he had had no choice but to let things play out. I told him, roughly, that, as an American, I had expected that the State Department had some kind of duty to try to keep its citizens OUT of trouble, not let them fall right into a life-threatening situation. He said something like how to handle things had all been decided from a level higher than his.

"Yes," I said, "at the Great Communicator's script writers' highest level. What they have done is to contrive a need that did not exist in order to have their lackey actor appear to be supremely masterful of an imaginary situation. What's next, an actual U.S. military invasion of one of these innocent islands, in the name of democracy, or the rescue of what? Maybe some med students at one of these fly-by-night schools?"

I left abruptly, telling him that the higher level needed to know that some probably innocent Americans did not make it out, that some, including seven real nurses, were even under arrest, even in dungeons, and probably would just vanish thanks to whatever bullshit official policy was being tested.

The final thing I told the consulate official on Antigua was that the next time I went to the Caribbean I would do it the way that my acquaintance, Harry Tubbs, back in Louisiana had done things, take a private army with him. The agent's face dropped, probably because he had heard of Harry's exploits in El Salvador and finally realized that a real private army would not have allowed themselves to get set up like the so-called "invaders" had, and that playing games with true Americans was severely "ill-advised."

Upon my arrival back in New Orleans I found that my child had indeed been severely injured. He had gone home from school and tried to emulate a science experiment that the teacher had demonstrated, opening a dry cell to see its inner components. Unfortunately he had punctured an alkaline battery which squirted the caustic gel into his eye. Joyce, the babysitter, heard his screams and immediately placed his face under the faucet, holding the struggling boy in place rinsing and flushing the eye for several minutes before releasing him so she could telephone his mother about the accident.

The eye doctors were all out of town at an annual convention. The on-call doctors had seen what I saw, which was an eye that looked like egg whites. It did look like the prognosis was going to be simply removal of the eyeball. The doctors agreed that such an action could wait for the return of the specialists.

I told the Creator that I knew that only such a thing could have gotten me to turn around and come back from the Caribbean instead of just heading down to St. Lucia to work for Dr. Bob, which had been my plan once things had gone so wrong on Dominica. I told the Creator that I had gotten the message, I was not to bail out of Louisiana, after all, there was too much responsibility at home that I had no right to shirk. I begged Him to heal my son, that it had not been my son's fault that I had failed. I begged the Creator to never again do to my children anything just to get me to obey what I should be able to understand to be my duties. I told Him to do it to me instead if I ever again decided to bail out or avoid some job He sent my way. I told Him to just put the step in front of me, whatever it might be, and that if I saw a step that needed to be taken, that if no one else could or would take it, that I would take it, knowing that He would punish me, just me, if I did not obey. I gave my boys the little bamboo boat.

The Creator healed my son. Within a couple of days, when the eye doctors returned and looked at the damaged eye, they decided to let it sit for another couple of days because it seemed to be changing from the original hopeless description. Within a week the eye had regained its structure, miraculously. The iris became visible, the cornea cleared up, the pupil let in the light...my child could see again. I praised the Lord of All Matter and Energy.

EPILOGUE

———

I did later, more than once, fail the Creator, and He has, each time, held me to the deal. I smile at how real it has been, the bailouts followed by the cancers... Yes, I smile because I know that He is real and the deal is real. May I never again weaken.

I have also failed the people of Dominica. I never got the visiting medical teams lined up. I never got the tire-retreading investigation started or completed. I never got the laundromat for the ladies who scrubbed clothes on the rocks by the rivers. I never got the fruit-for-rice shuttle set up between Portsmouth and Lake Charles. I never got the shipload of shoes to take to the Rastafarians and I never sent thousands of tourists to the Indian Rivermen... I simply never gained enough ground to make any of those things happen even though I did not bail out of my Louisiana calling.

I do somehow have hope that some of those things may yet be made to happen. It is the same kind of hope I retain for things like maybe yet getting to see, somehow, the "emerald drop." I cannot believe that such simple goals are beyond human reach.

I know that, in the Dominica misadventure, my own frailties got in the way, but I also still believe that the supernatural forces of evil meddled, maybe as tools for the Greater Good's Plan, but meddled nonetheless. I hope that the Greater Good will someday be fully independent of what is the lesser, the least, the evil.

I regret that my conversation with the State Department men on Dominica and back at the consulate in Antigua apparently had no effect. The same administration during which "Operation Red Dog" evolved did indeed proceed to develop a more sophisticated and even official invasion of a Caribbean island, Grenada, ostensibly to rescue Americans and fight evil. That effort was apparently championed by a fully convinced Ms. Eugenia Charles. Given the whipsawing policies that sling out from the United States from one year to the next, it is no wonder that the rest of the world views us as hypocritical imperialists.

I think back, from time to time, to my conversation with Emerson Watty. I think of how we had discussed things that might bring help to the children and things we did not see coming, like the Internet. I think of a central concept we did discuss: that the Creator might have allowed social hell to exist in such a natural paradise so that the world could someday see a model restoration of human dignity and peace and harmony, all things that should be inevitable in a place with such an overpowering and orderly natural ecosystem, a true Eden.

I ask again, "Whose fault is it that nothing seems to work on Dominica, nothing except Nature and its greatest adversary? What force steps into every good situation and turns it to chaos? What force seems to be able to command and destroy yet never show itself? Whose fault is it that real, advanced humans are so fully overwhelmed by invisible, inhuman, horridly evil and absolutely unreal primitive forces, unreal except in the minds of people and their governments? Whose fault is it anywhere on earth?"

I am still convinced that, "If there is a place where we can find out, it is Dominica."

We can smoke out the spirits of superstition and greed. We can destroy fear and selfishness.

I could have answered the Diablotin Jzhombie's question: "Do you know yet why you are here?"

I knew. I had found the doorway to hell. Once that doorway is shut behind him...

Dominica needs an Archangel who, with merciful restraint, will ask the Creator to rebuke the devils and imps that have enslaved Sunday Island, a darkened Paradise, Dominica, the Nature Island of the Caribbean.

Dominica can become that world model of diligent human movement toward perfection. Dominica has the base conditions that make possible the creation of that positive model that the rest of the earth's peoples could follow instead of repeating America's collapsing negative model of mistakes. So far, the world's nations are not learning from our country's having sacrificed the old, renewable resource based way of life for new ways of death.

Let the 1981 Dominican and 1983 Grenada fiascos be the last times the United States' "someones" think they know better than the islanders what is best for their own islands.

Recently I saw the beautiful Indian River mangle trees in a new pirate movie. I saw on the Internet the beautiful new tourist facilities that are spread all over Dominica. It is obvious that the good spirit on that island has not been vanquished.

I saw that the Rastafarians are creating a dialogue to remedy prejudices exacerbated by a law called "The Dread Act" which had been fostered by a Dominican man, Patrick John. I also learned that Patrick John had been picked (by or for) the Operation Red Dog ("Bayou of Pigs") KKK invaders as the figurehead they would install if their invasion of Dominica had been successful. Eighteen-wheelers I never saw… ones that ran over me…

I'm sure that it does still rain on Dominica, almost all the time, but let that rain always be the refreshing kind, nourishing the seeds of loving spirits, not the kind of spirit-drowning inundation born of the dark clouds of evil superstitions. Let the spirit of Jah prevail.